A
Challenge
to the
Critics

A
Challenge
to the
Critics

Scholarly Evidences of the
Book of Mormon

Diane E. Wirth

Copyright © 1986
Horizon Publishers & Distributors, Inc.

All rights reserved. Reproduction in whole or any
parts thereof in any form or by any media without
written permission is prohibited.

ISBN: 0-88290-312-8
Library of Congress Catalog Card Number: 85-081726
Horizon Publishers' Catalog and Order Number: 1011
First Printing, August, 1985

Printing: 2 3 4 5 6 7 8 9 10

Printed and distributed
in the United States of America by

Horizon
Publishers
& Distributors, Incorporated
P.O. Box 490 Bountiful, Utah 84010-0490

All views expressed in this book are those of the author and not necessarily those of any society, organization, or other affiliation with which the author is associated

Acknowledgments

This book expresses my personal findings as well as those of others who have spent hundreds of hours correlating recent archaeological, anthropological, literary, and theological findings relating to Book of Mormon claims.

I express my sincere gratitude to the following people and organizations. To John Sorenson, chairman of the Department of Anthropology, Brigham Young University, whose unrivalled knowledge on plausible Book of Mormon geographic sites gave me new insights on this subject during a F.A.R.M.S. trip to Mexico and Guatemala in June of 1984; to Bruce Warren, an expert in analysis of Mesoamerican historical accounts, who found my chapter on Quetzalcoatl "useful and interesting"; to V. Garth Norman, author of *Izapa Sculpture*, who found my observations on Stela 5 at Izapa, Mexico, "interesting" and "well done," giving me further insight on the subject. Also my thanks to him for permission to use his illustration of Stela 5; to Kirk Magleby, who painstakingly reviewed my first manuscript, who gave many helpful suggestions and exclaimed that I was "a good bloodhound"; to Paul Cheesman for his photograph of the Korean plates and his encouragement over the past years; to John Welch for his expertise on chiasmus, on both the F.A.R.M.S. *Tour to Book of Mormon Lands*, and his several articles on the subject; to Ron VanLeuven for his comments on my manuscript with regard to scriptural references; to George Carter for an update on the chicken in pre-Columbian times; to Gordon F. Ekholm for his positive view of the saddle-type object straddling a possible horse; to Duane Crowther, president of Horizon Publishers for his editorial critique and format suggestions; and to the following publishers, museums and universities for permission to use illustrations and photographs: Crown Publishers, New York; Musee de l'Homme, Paris; Dumbarton Oaks, Washington, D.C.; American

Museum of Natural History, New York; Museum fur Volkerkunde, Basel, Switzerland; Smithsonian Institution, Washington, D.C.; Deseret Book Company, Salt Lake City; The Society for Early Historic Archaeology, Provo; University of California, Berkeley; Peabody Museum of Archaeology and Ethnology, Harvard University; Princeton University; Stanford University Press; and the Newberry Library, Chicago. I also thank my family for their patience and support over the many years I conducted research for this project.

I take full responsibility for what is presented in this book. The results of my personal research have not been officially endorsed by The Church of Jesus Christ of Latter-day Saints or any other organization or individual.

Contents

Illustrations

Chapter 1

Answering the Critics

The Book of Mormon was published in 1830. Ever since, anti-Mormon critics have attempted to repudiate the book's authenticity. Statements and conclusions drawn by these critics are often based on inaccurate or incomplete information. Recent archaeological finds and results of various studies will be discussed to challenge those arguments and to support the contention that the Book of Mormon record of ancient Americans is, indeed, authentic.

Point

The Book of Mormon, a nineteenth-century translation by Joseph Smith, is a pre-Columbian compilation of records engraved on metallic plates by certain men and their descendants who came from the Old World.

Reference: Book of Mormon title page, an account written by the hand of Mormon upon plates taken from the plates of Nephi.

Counterpoints

The Book of Mormon, according to its author Joseph Smith, derives from a text describing the history of the American Indian written in Eqyptian hiero-glyphs on gleaming plates of gold; this record had been compiled in the period 600 to 400 B.C.[1]

Some have even claimed that reputable archaeologists have used the Book of Mormon as a guide book in locating the ruins of ancient cities in Central America.[2]

---

1. Nigel Davies, *Voyagers to the New World*, (New York: William Morrow and Company, 1979), p. 141.
2. Hal Hougey, *Archaeology and the Book of Mormon* (Concord, California: Pacific Publishing Co.), p. 3.

Commentary

Book of Mormon writers claim that voyagers from the Old World came to the Americas in pre-Columbian times. Twentieth century researchers have found strong evidence of many such voyages which supports the claim that such a cultural diffusion actually occurred. We will discuss many of these voyages of discovery. It is important to note, however, that the Book of Mormon was not intended to be an archaeological guide but a spiritual message as is the Bible; like the Bible, many who study it have been able to substantiate claims concerning the Book of Mormon.

Scholars who adopt a standard research procedure generally begin with a theory then look for evidence to support it. Heinrich Schliemann, a nineteenth-century German archaeologist of great renown, followed this procedure when he looked for the city of Troy, basing his belief that there actually was such a place as mentioned in Homer's *Iliad*. No one had been able to prove its existence but Schliemann believed the city once existed. With unstinted perseverance, he finally found it.[3]

Theories are developed by men. Gospel principles are based on revelation given to chosen prophets of God. LDS researchers attempt to bring about a better understanding of correlations between the Book of Mormon and the tangible evidence that exists. Such researchers are not responsible for formulating Church doctrine. Critics would have the public believe that since LDS scholars are not in agreement on such topics as the "Lehi Tree of Life Stone, Stela 5" or the geographical area of the Book of Mormon, that Mormon doctrine, in general, lies on unstable ground. However, it must be made clear that such interpretations have nothing to do with established Church doctrine.

A familiar technique used by anti-Mormon critics is to attempt to pit one LDS scholar against the other, i.e., ". . . it is now quite obvious that Dr. Nibley does not accept Jakeman's work on Stela 5 . . .'"[4] Jerald and Sandra Tanner, in particular, have used this technique in a number of their books. They set up what almost appears to be a contentious dialogue between LDS scholars espousing their theories.

There is no doubt that this is done in an effort to show that members of The Church of Jesus Christ of Latter-day Saints are not

---

3. C. W. Ceram, *Gods, Graves and Scholars* (New York: Bantam Books, 1972), pp.34-48.

4. Jerald and Sandra Tanner, *Archaeology and the Book of Mormon* (Salt Lake City: Modern Microfilm Co., 1969).

unanimous in their opinions. What this logic ignores is the distinction between revealed doctrinal principles and theoretical ideas that
may be interesting to study but are not connected with a person's
salvation.

One area where there is a difference of opinion among LDS Book
of Mormon scholars is their individual theories as to where the Book
of Mormon story took place. In the early days of the Church it was
assumed that this geographical area encompassed the whole of North,
Middle, and South America whereas the Book of Mormon refers to
this territory only as the "land northward" and the "land southward."
Specific locations were never designated as Book of Mormon sites
although Joseph Smith's editorial in the *Times and Seasons* issue of
October 1, 1842, page 927, stated the following:

> Central America, or Guatimala [sic] [the whole of what we now call Central
> America was then known as Guatemala], is situated north of the Isthmus of
> Darien [Panama] and once embraced several hundred miles of territory from
> north to south. The city of Zarahemla, burnt at the crucifixion of the Savior,
> and rebuilt afterwards, stood upon this land.

Zarahemla, according to the Book of Mormon, was in the land southward. This statement would, therefore, disqualify South America as
the land southward.

As study on the subject has progressed over the years, most LDS
scholars involved with trying to locate these lands now support the
limited Tehuantepec theory: the lands north and south of the Isthmus
of Tehuantepec in Mexico would be, in the Book of Mormon, the nar-
row neck of land separating the land north from the land south. The
record does not, therefore, include the history of the entire Indian population, as critics would have the public believe.

We now know that, in ancient times, many peoples came to the
Americas from both the east and the west. Dr. Stephen C. Jett, a professor at the University of California, Davis, who has made a study of
pre-Columbian transoceanic contacts, finds this concept to be feasible.

> A minority of scholars, which has grown considerably since the Second World
> War, feels that important, even fundamental outside influences may have
> helped shape ancient America. . . . Since there is nothing to suggest signifi-
> cant diffusion between the high cultures of the two hemispheres by way of
> the Bering Strait, the question of interhemispheric contacts among these cul-
> tures is essentially one of transoceanic voyaging. . . . In recent decades, con-
> tinuing archaeological, historical, ethnographic, and experimental research
> has tended to alter scholars' perceptions of the abilities of early watercraft

and their navigators. . . . Cultivated plants have long been looked to as excellent evidence of transoceanic contacts—particularly those plants which could not have been carried by way of Bering Strait or by any plausible natural means.[5]

LDS scholars admit that there were other groups of people in Mesoamerica besides those referred to in the Book of Mormon. Dr. John L. Sorenson, chairman of the Department of Anthropology at Brigham Young University speaks on this subject as follows:

> Were there other people around? We have already seen, from the information in the Book of Mormon concerning the dimensions of the lands, that it discusses a territory only hundreds of miles long. That leaves lots of space in the Americas that could have held millions of people—those referred to by father Lehi when he assured his sons that even in their day other peoples were waiting in the wings, so to speak: "many nations would overrun the land" if they only knew of it (2 Nephi 1:8).[6]

It is also well to note that the Book of Mormon does not claim to record the history of all the cultures that inhabited the western hemisphere. Although other nations are briefly mentioned, only those of the Jaredite, the Lamanite/Nephite, and the Mulekite nations are discussed. It would be inappropriate to say no other people came to this choice land from other parts of the world (see figure 1.1). We do not have records from all these people to testify of their history but those we do have give us a glimpse of how they once lived. We can begin to envision the greatness that was theirs in ancient times.

As we shall see, anti-Mormon critics who are not well informed on up-to-date Book of Mormon research often make erroneous conclusions with reference to the content of the Book of Mormon. There are critics who regard the entire Indian population and all of North and South America as a part of Book of Mormon history. With reference to the first quoted Counterpoint by Nigel Davies in this chapter, it must be noted that Joseph Smith was not the author of the Book of Mormon, but its translator; that the plates were not written in Egyptian hieroglyphics but in reformed Egyptian, which consisted of "the learning of the Jews and the language of the Egyptians" (Mor. 9:32 and 1 Nephi 1:2); and that the record was compiled between 600 B.C.

5. Stephen C. Jett, "Pre-Columbian Transoceanic Contacts," *Ancient Native Americans*, ed. Jesse D. Jennings (W. H. Freeman & Co., 1978), pp. 593-595.

6. John L. Sorenson, *An Ancient American Setting for the Book of Mormon* (Salt Lake City: Deseret Book Company and F.A.R.M.S., 1985), p. 83.

Fig. 1.1. Various cultures of Mesoamerica portrayed in terracotta. *Top left*, Caucasian female, Guerrero, Pacific Coast; *top right*, Negro, Plateau of Mexico, Tlapacoyan; *center, Semitic-type bearded man, Tabasco*(?); *bottom left*, Caucasian girl, Veracruz; *bottom right*, Oriental head, Plateau of Mexico, Tlapacoyan (all in private collections). Drawing after photograph from *The Art of Terracotta Pottery in Pre-Columbian Central and South America*, by Alexander von Wuthenau (New York: Crown Publishers Inc.).

and A.D. 421, with a small additional book originating at the time of the Tower of Babel incident.

Some non-Mormon scholars and archaeologists indirectly support LDS contentions. Referring to the Preclassic period (2000 B.C. to

A.D. 300) in Mesoamerica,[7] which corresponds to the Book of Mormon period, Alfred Kidder, a prominent archaeologist, points out that these civilizations were "approximately on the level with, and in general extraordinarily like those of our own cultural ancestors of the ancient Near East."[8]

Dr. Cyrus Gordon, who at the time was chairman of the Department of Mediterranean Studies at Brandeis University, told the 20th annual symposium on the Archaeology of the Scriptures at Brigham Young University on October 10, 1970:

> I am speaking academically and am not qualified to speak on the Book of Mormon itself. If I were to do that I would study it for three years before commenting. But there are many points in archaeology in its favor.[9]

With reference to this subject, Alexander von Wuthenau, an art historian specializing in pre-Columbian art, wrote:

> In recent years a considerable amount of terracottas which show characteristic Semitic traits have been found at archaeological sites. These discoveries may eventually make it obsolete to regard as mere childish nonsense certain indications in the Book of Mormon regarding the presence of Jewish elements in ancient America.[10]

The particular period of history in Mesoamerica accounted for in the Book of Mormon was an important one spanning from approximately 600 B.C. to A.D. 420. Dr. Sylvanus Morley, who wrote extensively on the Maya, acknowledged this when he stated:

> Something fundamentally important took place . . . during the three or four centuries immediately preceding and following the beginning of the Christian era. Was the cultural impetus due to some outside influence, or was it of autochthonous origin? Perhaps we shall never surely know.[11]

This is precisely the time recorded in the Book of Mormon; a time when the inhabitants of the land not only had prophets to guide them, but a time when the people were highly educated, skilled in the arts and crafts and knowledgeable in government management. Many of

---

7. Mesoamerica covers those portions of Mexico and Central America in which there existed several pre-Columbian cultures—commonly referred to as the Mesoamerican civilization.

8. Alfred V. Kidder, in *id.* Jesse D. Jennings, and Edwin M. Shook, *Excavations at Kaminaljuyu, Guatemala*, Washington (1946), p. 160.

9. *Deseret News* (Church Section), October 17, 1970.

10. Alexander von Wuthenau, *The Art of Terracotta Pottery in Pre-Columbian Central and South America* (New York: Crown Publishers, Inc., 1965), p. 49.

11. Sylvanus G. Morley, *The Ancient Maya* (Stanford: Stanford University Press, 1969), p. 184,

these skills were not native to the land's early Mongolian settlers who were primarily food gatherers; they were brought with cultures who ventured across oceans and seas to the New World.

For over one hundred years The Church of Jesus Christ of Latter-day Saints has declared that the Book of Mormon was written by a remnant of Israel in ancient America. It is only recently that many qualified non-Mormon scholars are in accord with the concept of pre-Columbian transoceanic voyages.

As will be seen in the following chapters, this new theory of cultural diffusion has gained considerable strength. Artifacts and botanical evidence are continually being found that link the Old and New Worlds. Ancient stone sculptures, paintings, and terracotta pottery that depict bearded men with the aquiline nose typical of Semitic-type races, can in no way be construed as Indians of Asian descent. A Bablyonian-type cylinder seal found in Tlatilco, Mexico, along with numerous Mediterranean-style writings, are but a few examples of recently discovered items which help clarify the origin of some of these early Americans. Interlocking artifacts together as pieces of a puzzle, history can be visualized in a new light: the Book of Mormon takes its place as an authentic part of Mesoamerican history.

Conclusions

•A misrepresentation of facts not only lessens the critics credibility as a researcher, but is unfair to the public. Assumptions, on the part of the critic, are not always valid.

•LDS scholars may differ in their theories, but theories are not Church doctrine. The Book of Mormon was passed on to us as a spiritual guide, not as a geographical map to find archaeological ruins.

•Israelites were not the only ones to cross the ocean to the Americas in pre-Columbian times. Many non-LDS scholars support the contention that there were early transoceanic voyages from the Old World to the New World.

Chapter 2

The Smithsonian Statement

The Smithsonian Institution's nine-point two-page letter (summer 1982), entitled "Statement Regarding the Book of Mormon," explains why the Institution feels it cannot support the concept of pre-Columbian voyages to the New World. (This handout is mailed to those who request the Institution's opinion on the validity of the Book of Mormon.)

Point

In the Book of Mormon there are many observations regarding the types of animals, crops, and races of people that lived in early America. Evidence of many of these have been substantiated: some only recently.

References: Animals: 1 Nephi 18:25; Grains: Mosiah 9:9; Ancestry: Omni 14, 15, and 3 Nephi, Chapter 5.

Counterpoints

The following is a summary of the Smithsonian Institution's nine-point letter entitled "Statement Regarding the Book of Mormon":

1. The Smithsonian Institution has never used the Book of Mormon as a scientific guide and sees no direct connection between the archaeology of the New World and the subject matter of the book.

2. The physical type of the American Indian is basically Mongoloid, most closely related to the peoples of eastern, central, and northeastern Asia. Archaeological evidence indicates that ancestors of the present Indians came to the New World via the Bering Strait land bridge.

3. The first people to reach this continent from the East were the Norsemen who briefly visited the northeastern part of North America around A.D. 1000 and who then settled in Greenland.

4. None of the principal Old World domesticated food plants or animals (except the dog) occurred in the New World in pre-Columbian times. American Indians had no wheat, barley, oats, millet, rice, cattle, pigs, chickens, horses, donkeys, camels before 1492. (Camels and horses were in the Americas, along with the bison, mammoth, and mastodon, but all these animals became extinct around 10,000 B.C.)

5. Iron, steel, glass, and silk were not used in the New World before 1492 (except for occasional use of unsmelted meteoric iron).

6. Any contacts (between peoples) from the Old World to the Americas would have been accidental. It is by no means certain that even such contacts occurred. There were no contacts with the ancient Egyptians, Hebrews, or other peoples of Western Asia and the Near East.

7. No reputable Egyptologist or other specialist on Old World archaeology has discovered or confirmed any relationship between archaeological remains in Mexico and archaeological remains in Egypt.

8. No inscriptions using Old World forms of writing have been shown to have occurred in any part of the Americas before 1492 except for a few Norse rune stones which have been found in Greenland.

9. There are copies of the Book of Mormon in the library of the National Museum of Natural History, Smithsonian Institution.[1]

Commentary

Anti-Mormon critics often use the Smithsonian's "Statement Regarding the Book of Mormon" to aid their case against Mormonism. As is well known, the Smithsonian Institution has one of the world's finest collections of archaeological finds along with many fine researchers. Unfortunately, however, the Smithsonian has become the final word of authority for the answer to many people's questions regarding the Book of Mormon's authenticity. It must be remembered that scholars are not agreed on Book of Mormon evidence: many have different opinions from that of the Smithsonian.

A wide variety of scientific subjects are studied at the Smithsonian. Consequently, their knowledge is broad rather than highly specialized on many subjects, and as a source of information on Book of Mormon topics, many would not consider the Smithsonian to be "highly qualified" on the subject.

---

1. "Statement Regarding the Book of Mormon," prepared by the Department of Anthropology, National Museum of Natural History, Smithsonian Institution, Washington, D.C., SIL-76, Summer 1982.

Numbers 1 and 9 of the Smithsonian Statement are not points to be contended with here as they merely state that they have copies of the Book of Mormon in their library, but the book is not consulted in relation to Mesoamerican archaeology. Numbers 2 through 8, however, are concrete statements made by the Institution. These, although they are somewhat generalized, will be examined here, and refuted.

Evidence

Number 2: One of the Smithsonian's major contentions is that "the physical type of the American Indian . . . is basically Mongoloid," but scholars have found evidence to the contrary. For example, Andrzej Wiercinski, a Polish anthropologist, analyzed a great many skulls from major Mesoamerican sites and discovered a variety of races. He found the Ameridian stock to be composed of not only Asians but many with features "introduced by . . . migrants from the Western Mediterranean area." He also stated that "ancient Mexico was inhabited by a chain of interrelated populations which cannot be regarded as typical Mongoloids."[2]

Another point the Smithsonian Institution uses for their support against the theory of diffusion, and consequently the Book of Mormon, is the old "Bering Strait" argument, which unfortunately continues to hold its own in our classroom textbooks. It cannot be denied that some of the Indians' ancestors reached the Americas via the strait, but the diffusion theory is more complex than that. The many artistic representations and other sources of information that support transoceanic voyages must be considered. Certainly, the Bering Strait represents one avenue by which the Americas became populated, but only one: that many others exist cannot be ignored.

Dr. G. A. Matson, one of the most noted workers in the field of American Indian genetics, studied blood grouping and stated "The American Indians are not completely Mongoloid." Professor Earnest Hooten of Harvard not only agreed with Dr. Matson, but thought he saw Near Easterners as a racial component.[3]

---

2. Andrzej Wiercinski, "Inter- and intrapopulational racial differentiation of Tlatilco, Cerro de las Mesas, Teotihuacan, Monte Alban and Yucatan Maya," *Act as, Documentos y Memorias, 36a Congreso Internacional de Americanistas*, Lima, 1970. Lima: Instituto de Estudios Peruanos, 1972, pp. 232-248. See also *An Evaluation of the Smithsonian Institution "Statement Regarding the Book of Mormon,"* by John L. Sorenson, paper available through F.A.R.M.S. (The Foundation for Ancient Research and Mormon Studies, Provo, Utah.)

3. G. Albin Matson, et al., "Distribution of hereditary blood groups among Indians in South America. IV. In Chile, "*American Journal of Physical Anthropology*, 27 (1967):188. See also *Men Out of Asia*, by Harold Gladwin (New York: McGraw-Hill, 1947), pp. 63-65.

It is interesting to note that blood types of the American Indian do not correspond to those of east Asian peoples where most scholars theorize the American Indian have their roots. In fact, a more plausible theory is that their ancestors came, by sea, from non-Mongoloid parts of the Old World. Blood types are genetically inherited and passed from father to son, from one generation to the next. Among Asians, blood types A and B are most common; among American Indians, blood type O predominates. Except for the Eskimos, and some Athapascan groups such as the Apache and the Navajo, blood group B is virtually nonexistent among American Indians throughout North, Middle, and South America.[4]

In essence, what we have is a chain of interrelated populations which cannot be regarded as typical Mongoloids. Artifacts found in the area of the Bering Strait suggest the influence of a rather small number of Asians—far below any number that would have been needed to produce the large populace which existed. What explanation do we have for other racial types in the Americas such as the Negro, shown in figure 2.1, if we follow current theories and refuse to consider transoceanic voyages?

Number 3: The first group of ancient mariners to have reached the Americas according to the Smithsonian's prepared handout was the Norse, around A.D. 1000. But the author who represents the Smithsonian in this statement appears to have overlooked numerous findings listed in a book in their own suggested reading list. This compilation of writings on contacts between Old and New World civilizations is entitled *Man Across the Sea: Problems of Pre-Columbian Contacts,* C. L. Riley, et al., University of Texas, Austin 1971. Several pro-diffusionist papers appear in this publication.[5]

---

4. See "North American Genesis," by Francois Eustache, *Frontiers of Science*, Vol. III, No. 3 (March-April 1981), Washington, D.C., p. 19; and *Genetics and the Races of Man*, by William C. Boyd, Boston (1950) p. 21.

5. Significant books and articles proposing transoceanic voyages to the Americas in pre-Columbian times are:

"Pre-Columbian Transoceanic Contacts," by Stephen C. Jett, *Ancient Native Americans*, ed. by Jesse D. Jennings, W. H. Freeman and Co. (1978); *Transoceanic Crossings to Ancient America*, ed. Ross T. Christensen, Brigham Young University, Provo; "The Transpacific Origin of Mesoamerican Civilization: A preliminary Review of the Evidence and Its Theoretical Implications," by Betty J. Meggers, *American Anthropologist*, Vol. 77:1 (March 1975); "On Pre-Columbian Discoveries of America," by George F. Carter, *Anthropological Journal of Canada*, Vol. 19, No. 2 (1981); *Fair Gods and Stone Faces*, by Constance Irwin, St. Martin's Press, New York; *Unexpected Faces in Ancient America*, by Alexander von Wutheneau, Crown Publishers (1975); *The Seafarers: Pre-Columbian Voyages to America*, by Frances Gibson, Dorrance & Co., Philadelphia (1974); "Pre-Columbian Voyages to the New World," by Larry J. Pierson, *Cabrillo and His Compatriots*, ed. by Dr. James R. Moriarity, III, 4th Annual Cabrillo Festival Historic Seminar, Vol. 1, No. 4 (1977).

Fig. 2.1. Water carrier, ceramic. From Teotihuacan, Mexico. (National Museum of Anthropology, Mexico.)

Number 4: The Smithsonian lists a variety of crops, animals and other items which they claim did not exist on the American continent before 1492. These things are not all mentioned in the Book of Mormon as one would suspect from reading this statement. This would also hold true for oats, millet, and rice; pigs[6], donkeys,[7] and camels. If it was the Smithsonian's intent to prove that transoceanic voyages

6. The word "pig" does not appear in the Book of Mormon; however, the word "swine" does. Boar lived in ancient Mesoamerica as they do today. See *The Olmec World*, Ignacio Bernal, University of California Press (1976), pp. 20, 123.

7. Although the Book of Mormon makes reference to the ass (1 Nephi 18:25), this does not necessarily mean the donkey. The ass can be one of several hardy, gregarious, quadruped mammals that are smaller than a horse and that have long ears: this includes the donkey.

did not take place because certain items were not transported from the Old World, their argument is weak indeed. Rice and camels were not found in Europe, yet cultures who did make use of them were close neighbors to the Europeans. And although the area which is now Texas was certainly close enough, geographically, for the people of ancient America to be acquainted with ancient Mexican architecture, none of the Aztec or Maya stepped pyramids have been found in Texas. Therefore, this argument is irrelevant. Close cultures do not mean shared cultures. Nor is there any reason why a group of Israelites would have brought to this land everything that was common to them in the Old World.

Items mentioned in the Smithsonian statement that would apply to the Book of Mormon have, in some instances, been found to have existed in pre-Columbian times. (See chapter 5 for discussion of elephants and horses.) Mesoamerican archaeology is still in its infancy. There is much yet to discover.

Barley, for example, is one of the items the Smithsonian claims did not exist in ancient America. However, in Phoenix, Arizona, at a Hohokam site (300 B.C. to circa A.D. 1450), barley was found in abundance; barley that was grown domestically.[8]

The Nephites did grow barley. Joseph Smith certainly could not have known whether barley was grown on this continent before the time of Columbus. Apparently the Smithsonian was not aware of this in 1982 when they made their statement.

And, yes, even the lowly chicken had its place in Mesoamerica. Dr. George Carter of Texas A&M University has pieced together several factors that indicate chicken was present in Mesoamerica in pre-Columbian times. He has seen chicken bones in Pecuni, Pueblo, circa A.D. 1400, and he states that evidences of chicken are often found since then. Dr. Hargraves told Carter that fourteen such finds have been identified in this area.[9]

Number 5: Iron, steel, glass, and silk are referred to in the Book of Mormon, but such references are not as cut and dried as they might appear to be. For example, an item such as "silk," mentioned in Alma

---

8. See "Last Ditch Archaeology," by Daniel B. Adams, *Science 83* (Dec. 1983), p. 32. With reference to other domesticated crops, see "Domesticates as Artifacts," by George F. Carter, *The Human Mirror. Material and Spatial Images of Man*, Miles Richardson, ed., Baton Rouge: Louisiana State University Press (1974), pp. 201-230.

9. George F. Carter, "Pre-Columbian Chickens in America," in *Man Across the Sea: Problems of Pre-Columbian Contacts, op. cit.*, pp. 178-218: Letter from Dr. George F. Carter to Diane E. Wirth, May 1985.

4:6 and Ether 9:17, presents a unique situation. Did Joseph Smith's use of the word "silk" mean that silkworms from China were actually found in ancient America? This is doubtful. But perhaps Joseph Smith used a word familiar in his time that would best describe a fine-textured fabric mentioned in the Book of Mormon for which we would have no name. In fact, there was a wild silkworm in Mexico whose spinnings were used by the Indians to make a fine material. They also wove the silky hair of rabbits into their fabric which resulted in a texture resembling the silk we are familiar with.[10]

Use of the word "silk" in the Book of Mormon is a prime example of a word used to more closely identify something we of today are familiar with. Thus the "steel" mentioned in the Book of Mormon may or may not have been forged the same way that the steel of today is forged. Steel differs from cast iron by its greater malleability and lower carbon content. In any case, both steel and iron readily rust in moist air, and many artifacts made of iron have been found to crumble when touched.

As for smelted iron, a famous Swedish archaeologist, Sigvald Linne, believes smelted iron was produced in a pottery vessel at Teotihuacan, Mexico. It was also Linne who found a piece of smelted iron in a tomb at Mitla, Oaxaca, Mexico.[11] Yet, according to the Smithsonian, no smelted iron was found in Mesoamerica.[12]

This leaves us with the use of the word "glass" in the Book of Mormon (Ether 3:1). This word is found only in the Book of Ether, and refers to a time before the Jaredites (the earliest Book of Mormon culture), arrived in the New World at the time of the Tower of Babel incident. Glass was certainly known in the Old World, even as early as 3000 B.C.

Every artifact found—a find which may be compared to the difficulty of finding a needle in a haystack—is probably representative of hundreds of others not yet discovered. But the finds that are made constantly update our scientific knowledge of Mesoamerica and, consequently, our scientific theory. Many things that were not proven

---

10. See I. W. Johnson, "Basketry and Textiles," *Handbook of Middle American Indians*, Robert Wauchope, et. al., eds., Vol. 10, Part 1, Austin: University of Texas Press (1971), p. 312.

11. "Mexican Highland Cultures," *Ethnographical Museum of Sweden, Stockholm, Publ.* 7, n.s., 1942, p. 132; and "Zapotecan Antiquities," *Ethnographical Museum of Sweden, Stockholm, Publ.* 4, n.s., 1938, p. 75.

12. See also "Metal Artifacts in Prehispanic Mesoamerica," by David M. Pendergast, in *American Antiquity* (1962), 27:520-544; and, *An Ancient American Setting for the Book of Mormon*, by John L. Sorenson, Deseret & F.A.R.M.S. (1985), pp. 284-286.

to exist in Joseph Smith's time are known in our era, and give strong support to the authenticity of the Book of Mormon.

Number 6: Interested scholars are gathering increasing amounts of data to support the presence of Semitic peoples in ancient America. Artifacts portraying bearded men with aquiline nose are in abundance as shown in figures 2.2 through 2.5. To date, literally hundreds have been documented.[13] The people represented in these sculptures cannot, in any way, be construed to be descendants of a Mongoloid race who crossed over the Bering Strait land bridge. The sculptures give mute evidence that Semites did migrate from the Old World to the New World as the Book of Mormon claims they did.

Indians do not grow beards—this is a genetic fact. Either the men have no beards or they have only a few sparse hairs. The rest of their bodies have much less hair than do American Caucasians.[14] So how are the numerous sculptures, the stone bas reliefs, the terracotta portraits of bearded Indians explained? Are they true "Indians," as these early Americans were called?

Kirk Magleby has done a statistical analysis of more than 230 bearded figures in Mesoamerica and found a remarkably even distribution of them throughout this area. Although bearded figures date from all time periods of the pre-Conquest era, Magleby found that they were much more frequent during Book of Mormon times. This coincides quite well to the period called pre-Classic by archaeologists, approximately 2300 B.C. to A.D. 300. By the time of the Aztecs, conquered by the Spanish in A.D. 1521, such portrayals of the beard were relatively rare.[15]

Several Mexican codices[16] depict leaders with appended false beards (figure 2.6), apparently an important feature of the elite. The Indians took pride in their ancestral heritage and false beards were symbolic of greatness and royalty. This was not unlike men of the Jewish culture in the Old World who considered a man's beard a sign of dignity and honor. By the time of the Conquest, the genetic makeup of races descending from Book of Mormon times had been so mixed they could no longer grow rich, full beards as their fathers did; and

---

13. See "A Survey of Mesoamerican Bearded Figures," by Kirk A. Magleby, available through F.A.R.M.S. [see footnote 2].

14. See *The Ancient Maya,* by Sylvanus G. Morley, 3rd ed. (1956), Stanford University Press, p. 23.

15. Magleby, *op. cit.*, p. 35.

16. Accordian-style folded manuscripts.

Fig. 2.3. Maya dignitary on onyx bowl. Bliss collection, Dumbarton Oaks, Washington, D.C.

Fig. 2.2. Bearded man, incense burner from Maya zone at Iximche, near Chimaltenango, Guatemala. Reproduced from *Discoveries of the Truth* by Diane E. Wirth, 1978. (Photo courtesy of Musee de l'Homme, Paris.)

Fig. 2.4. A bearded figure from the Rio Balsas, Guerrero, Mexico. (Neg. #274381, courtesy Dept. Library Services, American Museum of Natural History.)

Fig.2.5. Bearded man, Aztec culture. (Reproduced after photograph, Museum fur Volkerkunde, Basel, collection Lukas Vischer.)

Fig. 2.6. Bearded Mixtec warrior (after the Codex Nuttall).

in order to preserve this traditional heritage of their ancestors, they chose a false beard as a symbolic manifestation of high rank.

It is true, there is far more evidence of smooth-skinned Indians than there are of those having beards, but the Book of Mormon is a record of a small group of people who lived in a large land. This is in keeping with the number of bearded figures found, for the Nephites were well-known in all parts of Mesoamerica (Helaman 3:8), even though their numbers were less than those of the Lamanites who joined forces with any who would support their cause. The Lamanites would have, therefore, lost their Israelitish identity much sooner than did the Nephites who, as a rule, married other Nephites.

An obvious decline in the number of bearded figures took place at the close of the pre-Classic period, precisely when the Nephite civilization collapsed [circa A.D. 385].[17]

Many scholars admit to a lack of understanding of how these bearded "un-Indian" sculptures fit into Mesoamerican history. Others have recognized a real problem with these finds and choose to deal with it. Alesander von Wuthenau, one such scholar, has made an extensive study of pre-Columbian terracotta figures to identify early races of the Americas. He writes on this sensitive subject as follows:

> The interpretation of archaeological finds, their hypothetical explanation, is sometimes a delicate affair which many scholars dare to tackle only in a timid way, or not at all.[18]

However, von Wuthenau speaks up—no holds barred.

> I began an intensified study of pre-Columbian terracotta heads . . . what I was looking for were typical "Indian" heads. It was not long, however, before I discovered that in the early, lower levels these "genuine Indians" were not to be found. The earliest figures encountered were those with Mongoloid characteristics and . . . all kinds of white people, especially Semitic types with and without beards. . . . What is considered to be genuine Indian only developed, so far as I am able to judge on the strength of these terracotta representations, in early and middle Classic times, and probably derived from earlier types.[19]

From this we may surmise that early America became a melting pot of races, and that the so-called "Indian" type did not emerge until approximately A.D. 300, towards the end of Book of Mormon times.

Are we to believe that a genetic fluke took place in Mesoamerica which caused Indians to suddenly grow beards? Of course not. There has to be a logical explanation: the Book of Mormon gives a plausible answer to the dilemma.

Number 7: Although the people of the Book of Mormon who lived circa 600 B.C. were familiar with Egyptian ways (1 Nephi 1.2;

---

17. Magleby, *op. cit.*, p. 42.

18. Alexander von Wuthenau, *The Art of Terracotta Pottery in Pre-Columbian Central and South America* (New York: Crown Publishers, Inc., 1969), p. 42.

19. *Ibid.*, p. 49.

Mosiah 1:4; Mormon 9:32), they themselves were not Egyptian: they were Hebrew. How much the Egyptian culture influenced the art-work of this Israelite culture is not known, nor is it known whether or not they brought any artifacts from Egypt with them to the New World. But let us suppose they did. Are there scholars who believe there is a Mesoamerica/Egyptian connection? Yes, there are. As already pointed out, many pre-Columbian portraits depict men wearing false beards—some date to B.C. times. This was also a custom among Egyptian men.[20] The Egyptians deformed the heads of their infants who were born in royal households. So did the Maya. There are many other possibly significant traits peculiar to both cultures,[21] but among the most fascinating which deserve further investigation, are two Egyptian-style figurines on display at the Museo Nacional "David J. Guzman" in San Salvador, El Salvador.[22] These figures were found at a depth of three meters off an eastern beach near the Guatemala/El Salvador border. One figure depicts a man of noble lineage. The other is Osiris, the Egyptian god of death and resurrection. On both pieces are Egyptian heiroglyphs. These statuettes may prove to be very significant when further investigation in Central America is possible.

Reputable scholars are looking at several of these possible connections, but none has yet taken the bold step necessary to present a water-tight case for an Egyptian presence in Mesoamerica. As more discoveries are made the theory will no doubt gain support. If so, such discoveries will indirectly give additional credence to the Book of Mormon account.

Number 8: The author and representative of the Smithsonian letter under discussion states that "No inscriptions using Old World forms of writing have been shown to have occurred in any part of the Americas before 1492." This writer may not be aware of an important dig sponsored by the Smithsonian in 1891.

In March of that year Isaac Hooper found what appeared to be a grave headstone atop a wooded hill on his farm in Chatata, thirteen miles from Cleveland, Bradley County, Tennessee. Examination of the stone revealed letters and markings of an unknown origin.

---

20. Von Wuthenau, *op. cit.*, p. 138.

21. See *Ancient Egyptians and Chinese in America*, by R. A. Jairazbhoy, Rowman and Littlefield, New Jersey (1974).

22. See *Revista del Departamento de Historia*, I:3 (March 1930), p. 15; and "Two Figurines from the Belleza & Sanchez Collection," *F.A.R.M.S. Update*, January 1984 [see footnote 2].

Beneath the headstone was a partially exposed wall about two feet thick (depth and length excavated later). The curious inscription on the wall awed the scientific world.[23]

This historical site caused quite a stir from 1891 through about 1930 then appears to have been forgotten.

My first reaction when I learned about this find was, "Why isn't this inscription well-known in scientific circles?" Because of my interest in pre-Columbian transoceanic voyages and the many similarities of design between the Old and New World, I decided to delve into the mystery of this largely ignored discovery, and I spent two years in detective work. I determined to seek out all facts available.

The reason the site seems to have been forgotten is strange indeed. Shortly after it was discovered, Mr. J. Hampden Porter, acting in collaboration with the Smithsonian Institution, was assigned to investigate this unique discovery. He described the wall as an ancient construction of unusual design and proportion. The whole course of the wall ran 1060 feet in a semi-circular direction and was marked on the surface by stones 25 to 30 feet apart. It was composed of red sandstone and appeared to be three-ply, or three sections cemented together with a dark red cement-type mortar. The inscribed portion was found at the north end of the wall. It was eight feet high and sixteen feet long. Figure 2.7 shows the center layer of this portion of wall with an inscription containing 872 symbols or characters arranged in wavy parallel and diagonal lines.

Why was so little being done to investigate this site further? Shortly after J. Hampden Porter embarked upon the project, the Smithsonian Institution chose not to continue furnishing funds for the work. Was the Smithsonian short of funds, or too involved with other projects at the time? In Mr. Porter's letter of November 7, 1891, to the Smithsonian, he asked what happened to the two men with whom he had correspondence, the two men to whom he had sent photographs along with papers describing extensive research at the site. In this letter expressing his frustration to the Smithsonian Mr. Porter closed by saying, "It is certainly cut by man, but what race? Please reply at your earliest convenience since if I do not hear from the Smithsonian

---

23. See A. L. Rawson, "The Ancient Inscription on a Wall at Chatata, Tennessee," *Transactions of the New York Academy of Sciences*, Vol. 11 (November 9, 1891), pp. 26-28; A. L. Rawson, "The Ancient Inscription at Chatota, Tennessee," *American Antiquarian*, 14:221-223, July 1892; and *Sunday Sun*, New York, June 7, 1891.

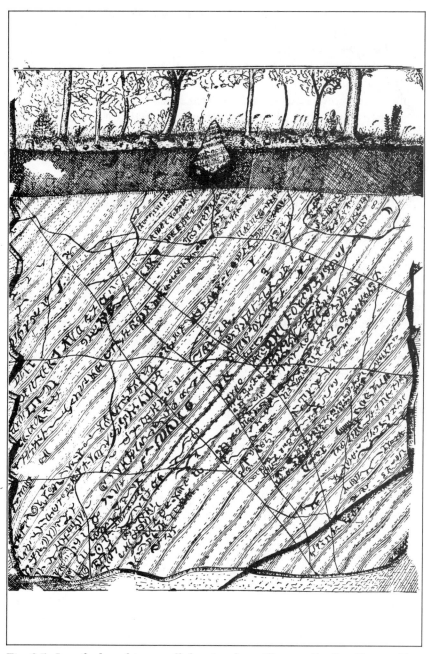

Fig. 2.7. Inscribed sandstone wall drawing from Chatata, Bradley County, Tennessee. Photo courtesy of Smithsonian Institution, Record Unit 6999T, Registrar, 1834-1958 (accretions to 1976), Accession Records, File #36766.

within a few days I shall leave this place without attempting to do anything more.[24]

There was no response.

Some years ago the Smithsonian told me that their linguist is of the opinion that certain marks on the Chatata inscription "have a vague similarity to known letters from the Near East."[25] Yet, to my knowledge, the Institute has done nothing further to investigate this site or the surrounding area.

Is there no significance in the growing accumulation of evidence?

Conclusions

•The Smithsonian Institution is not an authority on Book of Mormon cultures.

•Mexican and Central American Indians are made up of non-Mongoloid races as is evidenced by their blood type and by pre-Columbian sculptures of their ancestors.

•The Norse were not the only foreigners to settle in ancient America.

•Evidence of some grains, animals, and objects mentioned in the Book of Mormon have been discovered, some quite recently.

•Although not particularly relevant to the Book of Mormon, some Egyptian customs and artistic styles have been found in Mesoamerica.

•Some pre-Columbian races were literate and used scripts that had an affinity with Old World languages.

---

24. Letters and illustrations at Smithsonian Institution, Catalogue No. 205,857, Accession File 36766.
25. Letter dated September 10, 1979, from the Smithsonian Institution to Diane E. Wirth.

Chapter 3

Metal Plates and Stone Boxes

Although pre-Columbian scripts have been found throughout the Americas, the largest concentration of writing was found in Mesoamerica. There Indians inscribed their history in various ways in their art work, but more particularly on accordion-like manuscripts called codices.[1] Was the practice of record-keeping instilled in them by their ancestors from the Old World? The Hebrews were renowned for the careful way they kept their records. So were these early Mesoamericans. Semitic peoples also used various materials on which to inscribe their words. They even used metal plates as was done by the Book of Mormon record keepers.

Point

The bulk of the Book of Mormon, a companion scripture to the Bible, was written on metal plates by certain men in a colony of Israelites, descended from Joseph of Egypt. This method of record keeping was established by the forefathers of the Israelites. The tradition was continued in ancient America until about the fifth century A.D.

References: Plates of ore: 1 Nephi 19:1; Plates of brass: 1 Nephi, chapter 3; Plates of gold: Mosiah 8:9.

Counterpoint

He [the author, Martin Thomas Lamb, referring to himself] is compelled to believe that no such people as are described in the Book of Mormon ever lived upon this continent; that no such records were ever engraved upon golden plates, or any other plates, in the early ages.[2]

---

1. The names of some of the surviving codices are *Dresden Codex, Madrid Codex, Borgia Codex, Fejervary-Mayer Codex.* See *The Codex Nuttall,* ed. by Zelia Nuttall, Dover Publications, New York (1975), for paperback version of pictures and background regarding codices.

2. Martin Thomas Lamb, *The Golden Bible; or, the Book of Mormon. Is It From God?* (New York: Ward & Drummond, 1887), p.11.

Commentary

Hebrews in the Old World were known to engrave some of their records on metal plates. In fact, within the last fifty years, it has been discovered that people in many Old World cultures used metal plates; most of these plates have been found only recently. The history of the vast number of plates inscribed anciently cannot be covered in this writing, but some of the more important ones are listed below.

•Gold wafer, "Tablet of Shalmaneser III" (842 B.C.) from Kalat Shergat in modern Iraq (Oriental Institute, University of Chicago Museum)

•Gold and silver plates of Darius I, Persepolis (National Archaeological Museum, Tehran, Iran)

•Gold plate, Lambayeque, Peru (Hugo Cohen collection, Lima)

•Gold Plates, Pyrgi, Italy (500 B.C.) (National Museum of Villa Guilia, Rome)

•Rolled copper scrolls, Qumran, Dead Sea (2nd century B.C.) National Museum, Amman, Jordan)

•Small gold plate, "Djokha Umma" (2450 B.C.) (Louvre, Paris, France)[3]

The Book of Mormon was also engraved on metal plates—plates preserved in a stone box. Similar stone boxes have also recently been found throughout the world—in many cases, as a depository for metal plates.

Evidence

Joseph Smith was ridiculed by many because he claimed to be in possession of ancient records engraved on gold plates. A few unscrupulous people believed the story, on hearsay, and sought to take the records from Joseph for financial gain. Today, scores of ancient writings on metal plates have been found, but such records were anything but commonplace a hundred and fifty years ago. Even in scholarly circles the existence of these had rarely been heard of.

It is important to note that thousands of clay tablets have been discovered, as compared with fewer findings of metal records. Metal was used for records of great importance or to signify the financial standing of the record keeper.

---

3. Photographs of these plates can be seen in "Ancient Writing on Metal Plates," by Paul R. Cheesman, *Ensign*, October 1979, pp. 42-47.

In 1933, the Plates of Darius I were discovered. Darius was a Persian ruler from 518-515 B.C., and a near-contemporary of Lehi, a prophet from Jerusalem spoken of in the Book of Mormon. These Persian plates consisted of four metal tablets, two of gold, and two of silver. They were found deposited in stone boxes in Darius's palace at Persepolis as can be seen in figure 3.1. The marvelous quality about gold is that it does not crumble with age. These plates were as shiny and bright as the day they were placed in the stone boxes over 2500 years earlier. The message of the plates was befitting a king of Persia, declaring his majesty and the vastness of his empire.[4]

Another interesting find is the metal plates discovered in December, 1965, and referred to as the Korean Plates. Resembling a book, the sheets are hinged and folded on top of each other as seen in figure 3.2. The nineteen gold plates are inscribed with Buddhist scriptures and engraved with Chinese characters. They were also stored in a box (not stone, but bronze) and placed under a pagoda [circa A.D. 700] in South Korea. The Korean Plates are in the National Museum in Seoul.[5]

The Book of Mormon tells us that the keepers of their sacred records also used metal plates, a tradition that was carried with them from the Near East. After all, what better method was there than to inscribe characters on metal plates that would endure the rigors of time and be legible for centuries?

The Jaredites, the earliest civilization giving its history in the Book of Mormon, also left their records on gold plates for posterity (Mosiah 8:9; Ether 1:2). Since the Jaredites came from Mesopotamia at the time of the tower of Babel incident, finds of gold plates during their early period in the Old World would be significant. According to Richard Ellis, inscriptions on various types of metallic plates go back to as early as circa 2700-2500 B.C. in Mesopotamia.[6] Inscribing gold plates was therefore not unique to the Jaredite people: it was used by their contemporaries in the land from which they came.

Ancient plates were made of a variety of metals including gold, silver, copper, and bronze. The Book of Mormon prophet, Lehi, told

---

4. For a discussion on metal plates see "Ancient Burials of Metal Documents in Stone Boxes—Their Implications for Library History," by H. Curtis Wright, *Journal of Library History*, Vol. 16, No. 1, Winter 1981, University of Texas Press; Cheesman, *ibid.*

5. Cheesman, *ibid.*, p. 47.

6. Richard S. Ellis, "Foundation Deposits in Ancient Mesopotamia," *Yale Near Eastern Researches*, No. 2, New Haven and London: Yale University Press (1968), illustration 36.

Darius Plates.

Fig. 3.1. Darius plates. Reproduced from *Since Cumorah* by Hugh W. Nibley, 1970 edition. (By permission of publisher, Deseret Book Company.)

Fig. 3.2. Korean plates (photograph by Paul R. Cheesman in the National Museum, Seoul, Korea).

his sons to obtain a set of brass plates from Laban, who lived in Jerusalem. These plates recorded the history from earliest times along with a genealogy of the families of Laban and Lehi. These brass plates were eventually brought to the New World by Lehi, the chosen Israelite (see 1 Nephi, chapters 3-5).

As a rule brass deteriorates with time, but these records were preserved, perhaps because of the combination of copper, zinc, and possibly other metals in variable proportions used to make the plates. Bronze, which also has a copper base, has been found in the form of inscribed tablets from many ancient sites.[7] One in particular has

7. Wright, *op. cit.*

been dated to the sixth century B.C.; the same time the Book of Mormon states the plates of Laban existed. This bronze plaque was discovered in 1860 near Styria, Greece, and contained laws for the distribution of land. It is now housed at the National Archaeological Museum in Athens.[8]

Isaiah was commanded to engrave prophecy on brass.[9] Even earlier, during the time of Moses, the ancient Israelites used a kind of brass which was an alloy of copper and gold.[10]

The uniting of these two metals by the Israelites is interesting because we find the same combination used by early American smiths. We don't know the composition of the metal plates pertinent to our discussion, but it is very possible they were made of "tumbaga," an alloy of gold and copper commonly used by pre-Columbian metallurgists. The plates of the Book of Mormon had "the appearance of gold" but, since a chemical analysis was never made, we don't know what ratio of gold and/or other metals were used in the plates. Tumbaga would have made the plates lighter in weight than plates made of one-hundred-percent gold would be. For this reason alone, it would have served the Israelites well as the plates had to be transported from time to time.[11]

Metal plates, especially those engraved for the purpose of recording a people's secular and religious history, would have been preserved with great care. Nor would they be easily found. Since Mesoamerican archaeology has been minimal to date, compared to what needs to be done in vast areas, only one authenticated engraved plate containing Mayan glyphs has been found. This plate, discovered in 1950, was a gold disc taken from the sacred well at Chichen Itza on the Yucatan Peninsula. Around the disc's edge is a Mayan inscription. (The object is now in the Peabody Museum at Harvard University.) Many virgin metal sheets have also been found throughout Mesoamerica and South America.

Throughout the Americas, shortly after the Conquest, stories told by the Indians about metal plates used for keeping records also merit

---

8. Cheesman, op. cit., p. 47.

9. Isaiah 8:1 where the Hebrew text reads "take thee a great Gillayon and write in it . . . the word "gillayon" was observed by Dr. Adam Clarke, a celebrated Biblical scholar, to mean a polished tablet of metal upon which the prophecy was to be engraved.

10. Flavious Josephus, Antiquities, B XI, Ch. V, V. 2.

11. Read H. Putnam, "Were the Plates of Mormon of Tumbaga?" Papers of the Fifteenth Annual Symposium on the Archaeology of the Scriptures, BYU, Provo, Utah, May 16, 1964. See also "Tumbaga Object from the Early Classic Period, found at Altun Ha, British Honduras," by David Pendergast, Science, 168:116-118.

our attention. William Bolsover wrote about his dealings with the Ispogogee Indians at Tuckabatchee, Alabama. This tribe of priestly Indians had many brass and copper plates containing prophetic writings of their forefathers which were given to them by the same deity they say we call God.[12]

In their book, *America's Ancient Civilizations*, Hyatt and Ruth Verrill tell of a Maya book containing the complete history of their ancestors. This book is said to have been inscribed on gold plates. The Verrills write concerning this record.

> According to traditions a complete history of the Maya was recorded in the Golden Book of the Mayas which, if it actually existed, as it probably did, was so carefully hidden to prevent it from falling into the hands of the Spaniards that it never has been found.[13]

Harold Wilkins reported that the Indians of Chiapas, Mexico, claimed their people were in possession of a record written by their ancestors and engraved on gold leaves. This book was supposedly concealed in vaults of some ancient city at the time of the Conquest.[14]

Perhaps additional metal plates will be discovered in Mesoamerica some day. We know that the Book of Mormon is an abridgement of many records—possibly a condensed version of a whole library.

In many of the above-cited cases, the ancient metal plates discovered in our time were found to be stored in stone boxes as were the Book of Mormon plates. Joseph Smith was not only unaware of the use of metal plates in the Old World, but he could not have known that, after his death, more than fifty stone boxes would be found in Mesoamerica where much of the Book of Mormon story took place.

A variety of objects have been found in ancient American boxes, from jewelry and clothing, to tools, and—in one case—an ancient record. Robert Wauchope describes other stone boxes found in the late nineteenth century.

> On her deathbed, Alice Le Plongeon (wife of Augustus Le Plongeon) turned over to an intimate friend many of her husband's drawings and notes and evidently tried to tell the location of another spectacular discovery they claimed to

12. Edward King, viscount Kingsborough, *Antiquities of Mexico*, Vol. viii, pp. 357, 358 (London), James Moyes, 1831-1848.

13. Alpheus Hyatt Verrill and Ruth Verrill, *America's Ancient Civilizations* (New York: G. P. Putnam's Sons, 1953), p. 23.

14. Harold T. Wilkins, *Mysteries of Ancient South America*, Citadel Press, New York (1956), p. 180.

have made and covered again in 1875—some underground rooms containing stone boxes holding perfectly preserved ancient records of the Maya.[15]

It was obvious that these ancient boxes were used to store selected items of value to the people and that these boxes were sometimes buried with their dead. Many of these boxes, as shown in figure 3.3, are on display at the Museum of Anthropology in Mexico City. These finds from the past strengthen Joseph Smith's claim that plates of gold in a stone box was precisely the way he found the ancient American record of the Book of Mormon.[16]

Fig. 3.3. Stone box displayed at Museum of Anthropology, Mexico City. (Photo by Diane E. Wirth.)

15. Robert Wauchope, *Lost Tribes and Sunken Continents*, The University of Chicago Press (1962), p. 19.
16. On the subject of stone boxes, see also *These Early Americans*, by Paul R. Cheesman, Deseret Book Company (1974), Chapter 9.

Conclusions

•In the Old World there was a long tradition of concealing metallic documents in stone boxes.

•The plates of Darius, in particular, were prepared at about the same time that Nephi inscribed the history of his people on metal plates.

•Tumbaga, an alloy of gold and copper, was used in Mesoamerica and may have been used to make the plates on which the Book of Mormon was inscribed.

•Indians, at the time of the Conquest, were aware that their ancestors kept golden books.

•Stone boxes have recently been found in both the Old and New Worlds: boxes completely unknown in Joseph Smith's time and not discovered until many years after his untimely death.

Chapter 4

Nephite Monetary System

Most ancient coins of the Old World origin found in the Americas are determined to have been brought here after the Conquest. The Book of Mormon has been criticized on this basis; however, where in the Book of Mormon text is the word "coin" used?

Point

The Book of Mormon speaks of a monetary system used to pay wages and debts with various measures of gold and silver, or grain. This economic system was used by the Nephite people in particular. *References:* Alma 11:3, 5-19 and 22.

Counterpoint

What do we find when we look at the Book of Mormon? In Alma, 11th chapter, verses 5-19, is a listing of the coinage of the period of time that was used by the people. It lists the senine of gold, the seon of gold, the shum of gold. They had lesser coins, the shibom, the shiblum, the leah. Need it be said at this point that not one of these coins has ever been found?[1]

Commentary

Critics, and even some LDS writers, often assume that the monetary names used in the Book of Mormon refer to coins. However, nowhere in this record is the word "coin" mentioned.

Evidence

Money does not necessarily denote coinage. In fact, the Egyptians and Babylonians used pieces of metal in conventional shapes whose value was determined by their weight.[2] It is possible that the

---

1. Dr. Richard Fales, archaeologist and a narrator in the film, *The God-Makers*, Jeremiah Films.
2. Ed. Meyer, *Gesch. des Altertums*, (1909), I, ii, p. 517, cited in *Since Cumorah*, by Hugh Nibley, Deseret Book (1970), p. 255.

Nephites did not use coins, as we know them, and may even have employed another system used by the Egyptians which archaeologists refer to as "ring money." There may be other forms we are not aware of at this time.[3]

Paul Jesclard, who made a study of ancient monetary systems, found connections between the system used by the Nephites and similar systems used in the Near East. Before Lehi and his family came to the New World, they were familiar with Egyptian ways, as they were familiar with the language. Consequently, "they would have used the system every time they went into Egypt to do business and in turn would have taught it to their descendants in the New World."[4] This system is concerned with fractional measurements of grain: the two systems, oceans apart, correspond quite well.

From Alma 11:7 we know that certain amounts of silver and/or gold were equal to appropriate measures of various types of grain:

> A senum of silver was equal to a senine of gold, and either for a measure of barley, and also for a measure of every kind of grain.[5]

The field of linguistics also has a strong bearing on the issue at hand. Alma 11:22 refers to "onti," which is an Egyptian word meaning "small amount" or "short of an amount." If we take the word *senum*, referred to in Alma 11:3, we come up with an Egyptian word with a Nephite ending. Nephite endings to words were no doubt a grammatical device to change Egyptian words to their language. *Sen* in Egyptian means "one-half" or "doubling."[6] Jesclard noted "This would also tend to fit into the Nephite method, because a *senum* is doubled each time to make the next highest amount." *Limnah* (Alma 11:5), a gold standard, has not an Egyptian, but a Hebrew meaning of "to count or weigh."[7] These terms appear to be quite fitting since

---

3. See Paul Richard Jesclard, "A Comparison of the Nephite Monetary System with the Egyptian System of Measuring Grain," a paper read at the Twenty-first Annual Symposium on the Archaeology of the Scriptures, BYU, Oct. 16, 1971.

4. *Ibid.*

5. Domesticated barley has been discovered by archaeologists in Phoenix, Arizona (see "Last Ditch Archaeology," by Daniel B. Adams, *Science 83*, Dec. 1983, pp. 28-37). The ancient culture that lived here was called the Hohokam. Many characteristics of these people show a strong Mesoamerican influence and it is agreed among scholars that trade existed between this area and Northern Mexico. Alma 63:6-10 describes various Nephite migrations to the North which may give an explanation for the origin of barley in the region now called Arizona.

6. *Worterbunch der Aegyptischen Sprache*, IV, pp. 164-165, cited in Jesclard, *ibid.*

7. Francis Brown, S. R. Driver, and C. A. Briggs, "A Hebrew and English Lexicon of the Old Testament" (Clarendon Press: Oxford, 1968), p. 584; referred to in Jesclard, *ibid.*

we know that the Nephites used a combination of Egyptian and Hebrew in the language they referred to as "reformed Egyptian."

John Welch, professor at Brigham Young University's J. Reuben Clark Law School and president of the Foundation for Ancient Research and Mormon Studies, also made an interesting observation. In Alma 11:16 we come across a unit of measurement called *shiblum*. Checking an original fragment and printer's manuscript of the Book of Mormon, it was found that the word was actually *shilum*, not *shiblum*. *Shilum* just happens to be a Hebrew word meaning "payment, reward, or retribution."[8]

Since the monetary categories referred to in the Book of Mormon refer to measures, it is plausible to assume that various amounts were used to measure a number of trade items. Cacao beans, for example, were one of the most prized possessions in Mesoamerica. Their monetary value was calculated according to their number,[9] and—in larger quantities—by their measure.

Trade was very extensive in Mesoamerica, and, like the barter system, objects of value were used as money. Thompson tells us "Copper celts were used to a limited extent at the time of the Spanish Conquest and had a secondary use as a form of currency."[10] Although bartering was the aboriginal method of exchange, it still survives in many parts of Mexico today and plays a definite role in their economy.[11]

It can, therefore, be stated that the absence of "coins" per se in the Americas is irrelevant where it concerns the monetary system of measures of gold, silver, and grain used by the Nephites.

Conclusions

• The word "coin" does not appear in the Book of Mormon text.

• The Nephite monetary system is concerned with measurements.

• Several Nephite words for various weights and measurements have their origin in Egyptian and Hebrew words.

• Bartering of weighed and/or measured goods, be it of grain or metal, was considered a method of exchange in Mesoamerica.

---

8. See "Volunteers Team Up to Study Book of Mormon," by Sue Bergin, *BYU Today*, Feb. 1985, pp. 15, 16. Verified in letter dated 20 February 1985 from the Historical Department, The Church of Jesus Christ of Latter-day Saints to Diane E. Wirth.

9. J. Eric S. Thompson, *The Rise and Fall of Maya Civilization* (Norman: University of Oklahoma Press, 1954), p. 155.

10. Thompson, *ibid.*, p. 184, 185.

11. George M. Foster, *A Primitive Mexican Economy* (New York: J. J. Augustin Pub., 1942), p. 55.

Chapter 5

Elephants, Horses, and Bees
in Ancient America

The time period of the Book of Mormon is of such wide scope that it does not include many minute historical details. Yet references it makes to the elephant, the horse, and the bee have caused a great deal of controversy concerning the existence of these animals in pre-Columbian America. Despite skepticism by critics, scholars have found evidence to support the probability that all three did exist in ancient America.

Point

The Jaredites not only wrote their witness to the elephant, but they claimed the animal was of great use to them. Lehi's party found horses in the land of promise that was the Americas. The Book of Mormon also states that the Jaredites brought honeybees from across the seas.

References: Elephants: Ether 9:19; Horses: 1 Nephi 18:25, Enos 21, Alma 18:9-12, Alma 20:6, 3 Nephi 3:22, 3 Nephi 4:4; Bees: Ether 2:3.

Counterpoints

Elephants were extinct in America before the Jaredites could have gotten here![1]

It is now agreed that, while the horse was an inhabitant of America in the earlier geologic epochs, he ceased to exist long before man had attained to any considerable degree of culture as represented in the Book of Mormon.[2]

Bees are said to be in America about 2000 B.C. in Ether 2:3, yet they were first brought to the New World by the Spanish explorers.[3]

---

1. Gordon H. Fraser, *What Does the Book of Mormon Teach?* (Chicago: Moody Press, 1964), p. 90.
2. Charles A. Shook, *The True Origin of the Book of Mormon* (Cincinnati: Standard Publishing Co., 1911), p. 161.
3. Ed Decker and Dave Hunt, *The God Makers* (Eugene, Oregon: Harvest House Publishers, 1984), p. 113.

Commentary

The book of Ether in the Book of Mormon is a short account covering an extensive time period and does not, therefore, go into much detail. One interesting mention has been a source of contention, especially for those who would like to find fault with this record. According to the Book of Mormon, the Jaredites had elephants that were very useful to them. Man has always been fascinated with the thought that his predecessors hunted the great mammoth. The question is, however, how late in prehistoric times did the mammoth's relative, the elephant, roam the Americas?

The Book of Mormon also claims that there were horses in the land. Both the anti-diffusionist and the anti-Mormon critic insist that the horse did not exist either at the time of the Conquest or at any other time in the Americas—excluding a prehistoric pygmy horse. There are not many artifacts to support the theory that the horse lived during the period in question, but the data we do have is noteworthy. If the horse lived beyond the time most scientists speculate they did, what was the reason for their demise?

Was the bee in ancient America? A person unaware of existing evidence would not be certain that it was. Mesoamerican archaeologists would have to affirm that the bee did, indeed, exist in Mexico before the Spanish Conquest.

Evidence

The Elephant

Most researchers would not care to explore the subject of the elephant in ancient America because many scientists are of the opinion that there were no elephants in the Americas during this period (approximately 2500 B.C.). They do acknowledge, however, that mastodons and mammoths lived on the western hemisphere thousands of years before this time.

Some scholars have moved the date up to 3000 B.C.[4] Nor does the date of circa 2500 B.C. appear so unreasonable after we examine a little of the mounting evidence about the elephant in pre-Columbian—not prehistoric—times.

The eminent Austrian ethnologist, Dr. Robert Heine-Geldern, reported to one Dr. Clyde Keeler that there were five elephant

---

4. Ludwell H. Johnson, III, "Men and Elephants in America," *Scientific Monthly*, Oct. 1952, pp. 220-221.

effigies found in Mexico, but because they were not found by bona-fide archaeologists, professionals continue to disregard this controversial subject.[5]

Dr. Verrill, a well-known archaeologist who did fieldwork for the Museum of the American Indian, Heye Foundation, has not been afraid to express his opinions about this delicate subject. He describes a figure from Cocle, Panama, as follows:

> The most astonishing of the idols is one bearing a figure which is so strikingly and obviously elephantine that it cannot be explained away by any of the ordinary theories of being a conventionalized or exaggerated tapir, ant-eater or macaw. Not only does this figure show a trunk, but in addition it has the big leaf-like ears and the forward-bending knees peculiar to the elephants. Moreover, it shows a load or burden strapped upon its back. It is inconceivable that any man could have imagined a creature with the flapping ears and peculiar hind knees of an elephant, or that any human being could have conventionalized a tapir to this extent.[6]

Carvings of the elephant have also been found in such locales as Gallo Canyon, New Mexico; Glen Canyon, Colorado; Flora Vista, New Mexico; Cuernavaca, Mexico; and Cali, Columbia. Many of these are petroglyphs which, unfortunately, cannot be dated and will probably always remain open to criticism.

Even so, according to K. MacGowan, man-mammoth associations are numerous. In his book, *Early Man in the New World*, he lists twenty-seven places where remains of the beast and man were found together.[7]

Along with their remains, and artifacts depicting them, we have folklore of the elephant. Numerous legends told by Indians shortly after the Conquest referred to a large animal with an extremely long nose. These animals were seen by the ancestors of these Indians, and it seems that each generation told their children tales of this animal of monstrous proportions.

Ludwell H. Johnson is of the opinion that there can "no longer be any reasonable doubt that man and elephant coexisted in America." In his article, "Men and Elephants in America," he states:

---

5. Bubba Davis and Clyde Keeler, "The Georgia Elephant Disk," *The Epigraphic Society Occasional Publications*, Vol. 8, Part 2, No. 199, Nov. 1979.

6. Hyatt Verrill and Ruth Verrill, *America's Ancient Civilizations* (New York: G. P. Putnam's Sons, 1953), pp. 132, 133.

7. K. MacGowan, *Early Man in the New World* (New York: Macmillan, 1950), pp. 137-139, 142.

Archaeology has proved that the American Indian hunted and killed elephants; it has also strongly indicated that these elephants have been extinct for several thousand years. This means that the traditions of the Indians recalling these animals have retained their historical validity for great stretches of time.[8]

Referring to middle-American sculpture, J. Eric Thompson wrote:

In one or two cases the trunks are certainly very elephantine. The explanation is probably to be found, not in an Asiatic prototype, but in a half-forgotten tradition of the mastodon.[9]

The rain god of the Maya, referred to as "the long-nosed rain god," is often endowed with a pronounced elephantine proboscis, as seen in figure 5.1. It is well-known that the elephant can fill its trunk with water and spew it out. Was this Maya design of the rain god, so often portrayed in their codices (books), an accident? The record of the Jaredites claim that the elephants were here, in the Americas.

The Horse

Several curious artifacts and bas-reliefs in Mesoamerican art portray four-legged animals. At Chichen Itza, on the Yucatan Peninsula, for example, there is a bas-relief of a bearded man, shown in figure 5.2, who stands alongside what appears to be a horse.

Although there are those who claim this is a dog, when has anyone seen a Mexican dog almost tall enough to reach a man's shoulder—even a short man? It appears more reasonable that this

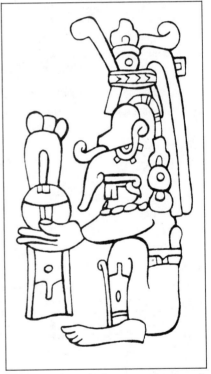

Fig. 5.1. Chac, the long-nosed rain god, Codex Tro-Cortesiano. From *Codices Maya* by Villacorta & Villacorta, Guatemala City: Tipografia Nacional (1930).

---

8. Johnson, *ibid.*

9. J. Eric Thompson, *Mexico Before Cortez* (New York: Charles Scribner's Sons, 1937), p. 290.

Fig. 5.2. Horse at Chichen Itza. (Courtesy of Mrs. Milton R. Hunter.)

"dog" is a small breed of horse. Robert Marx claims to have found frescoes of horses at a site near Chichen Itza "horses grazing, frolicking and running, some mounted with riders."[10]

In the more unexplored regions of the North States of Amazonia in Brazil, Professor Marcel Homet investigated some interesting petroglyphs at the Pedra de Beliquevem—petroglyphs that portray horses with and without riders, and some burdened with baskets. Although these stone carvings, called "petroglyphs," cannot be dated, many of the inscriptions at this and other nearby sites have been determined by scholars to be composed of ancient Mediterranean characters.[11]

Housed at the American Museum of Natural History is an interesting terracotta animal which once functioned as a wheeled toy, or funerary object. See figure 5.3. Seated upon this small animal is a man

---

10. Robert Marx, "Who Really Discovered America?", *Argosy*, (April 1973), Vol. 376, No. 4.
11. Marcel F. Homet, *Sons of the Sun* (London: Neville Spearman, 1963).

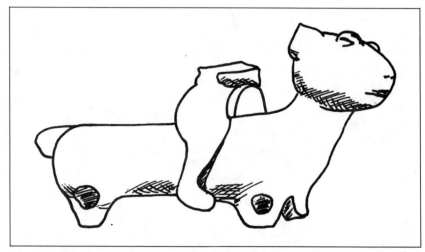

Fig. 5.3. Rider on animal with saddle. (After photograph [Ekholm, Plate XXVI] Cat. No. 30.0-3274, American Museum of Natural History.)

although the top half of the rider is missing. Dr. Gordon Ekholm of the Department of Anthropology of this museum showed the object to Dr. Ignacio Bernal, an expert in Oaxacan, ceramics, and he agreed "that it looks like a pre-Columbian object."[12] Dr. Ekholm makes an interesting observation of his own on this find.

> The really extraordinary feature is the rider, unfortunately incomplete, seated on the animal's back with legs clasping the sides of the animal in a manner exactly like that of a horseback rider. There are also clay fillets behind and in front of the rider which obviously represent some form of saddle.[13]

We find another interesting design of an animal from the pre-Conquest Mochica Period (A.D. 400 - A.D. 1000). This delightful animal is termed the *Strombus Galeatus* monster by archaeologists, as seen in figure 5.4. Ask any child which animal this is and chances are he will say "a horse." Late pre-Columbian cultures, before the Conquest, depicted this animal, perhaps by using descriptions from legends that originated with their ancestors. Closely resembling the horse in body, head shape, and hair of the mane, this animal is drawn with claws instead of hooves and the tail, although fringed with hair, is

12. Letter from Dr. Gordon Ekholm, The American Museum of Natural History, to Diane E. Wirth, June 27, 1977.

13. Gordon F. Ekholm, "Wheeled Toys in Mexico," *American Antiquity*, 11:224-226 (1946), Society for American Archaeology.

Fig. 5.4. Strombus Galeatus monster, Mochica. (After drawing from Bulletin 143, Bureau of American Ethnology, Washington, 1946).

thickened. On the back of the animal is a feathered shell reminiscent of the wings of Pegasus.[14]

These are a few illustrations given to support the theory that the horse did exist in ancient America. What we have to look for now is why the animal no longer roamed these lands at the time of the Conquest.

Researchers have determined that the ancient horse was hunted and eaten by early natives of South America.[15] In fact, horse meat is still eaten in Mexico today. In addition, historians have noted that in times of war and famine, the horse was used primarily as a source of food rather than a means of transportation.

---

14. Some of the information on the horse in this chapter was given by author at the 26th Annual Symposium of the Society for Early Historic Archaeology, BYU, in an unpublished paper entitled "Horses and Chariots in Ancient America," (1977).

15. Leo Deuel, *Conquistadors Without Swords* (New York: St. Martin's Press, 1967), p. 538.

In like manner, the Lamanites frequently sought to capture the cattle of the Nephites to sustain their own economy. Third Nephi 4:4, in the Book of Mormon, states that the Nephites were sorely plagued by armies of robbers [circa A.D. 19]. Consequently they left their lands desolate, taking with them provisions "and horses and cattle, and flocks of every kind, that they might *subsist* for the space of seven years." Now the word "subsist" means to have or acquire the necessities of life, such as food and clothing in order to survive. It is, therefore, reasonable to assume that, as a result of Lamanite rustling and the Nephite's need to sustain their people, the horse became extinct.

This extinction of the horse can be likened to the near-extinction of the bison in the early west. Hundreds of thousands of bison, more commonly called "buffalo," once roamed North America. Only the efforts of several conservationists saved this animal from extinction as well.

The bison is not the only good example of endangered or extinct animals. There are many references to lions in the Bible, yet the last Palestinian lion of record was killed in a hunt around A.D. 1100.

Today there are no so-called archaeological remains of lions in the land of Israel. Apparently not a bone has been left.[16] Therefore, a lack of skeletal remains of an animal in a particular area does not necessarily mean that the animal was never there.

The Bee

J. Eric Thompson wrote that not only was the domestic bee in ancient America but that there were gods of bees and beekeepers as depicted in figure 5.5.[17] Honey

Fig. 5.5. The bee god descending on a hive. (After Mayan Codex.) Honey and wax played an important part in Maya lives.

---

16. Benjamin Urrutia, "Lack of Animal Remains at Bible and Book-of-Mormon Sites," *Newsletter and Proceedings of the Society for Early Historic Archaeology*, No. 150, Aug. 1982.

17. J. Eric S. Thompson, *Maya History and Religion*, University of Oklahoma Press, 1970 (1976), pp. 152, 277.

was considered a real treat for the Indians. Equally important was black wax taken from the hives which was often traded for other commodities. The existence of the bee, anciently, is also supported by Ignacio Bernal whose specialty was the Olmec civilization.[18] (The Jaredite culture coincides with the name of the earliest grand culture of Mesoamerica, dubbed the "Olmec," an archaeological name given to these people meaning "Dweller in the Land of Rubber.")

Conclusions

•Scholars have presented evidence to show that the elephant existed into Jaredite times.

•Mesoamerican art pieces portray the elephant as described by the forefathers of the craftsmen.

•The horse is depicted in pre-Columbian stonework.

•Evidence has been found depicting a saddle-like object atop what is possibly a horse.

•The horse may have met its demise on the dinner table.

•No archaeologist would deny the existence of the bee in ancient America.

---

18. Ignacio Bernal, *The Olmec World*, University of California Press, 1976 edition, p. 20.

Chapter 6

The Wheel

Although the wheel was not in use in Mesoamerica when the Spanish arrived, ancient Americans obviously had knowledge of it. Although it was apparently used for decorative rather then utilitarian purposes, the wheel was still a part of Mesoamerican culture.

Point

It is recorded in the Book of Mormon that the Nephites and Lamanites used chariots during the period between 100 B.C. and A.D. 20.

References: Alma 18:9, Alma 20:6, and 3 Nephi 3:22.

Counterpoints

The chariots would, of course, suggest wheels. This is another gross blunder. The wheel was never used in America before the coming of the Europeans, and was not adopted by the Indians even after they had come into possession of the Spanish horses. . . . The wheel was never used in making pottery.[1]

The Diffusionist have never given any explanation of the absence of large-wheeled vehicles and of Old World beasts of burden in America. Would these powerfully useful instruments not have survived . . .?[2]

Commentary

Since their forefathers came from the Near East where wheeled chariots and other vehicles were well-known, it is logical to assume that knowledge of the wheel was retained by the Nephites. Alma, the son of Alma, and Nephi, the son of Helaman, assert that they made use of chariots (see references above). This has been interpreted by

---

1. Gordon H. Fraser, *What Does the Book of Mormon Teach?* (Chicago: Moody Press, 1964), p. 61.
2. George Kubler, "On the Colonial Extinction of the Motifs of Pre-Columbian Art," *Essays in Pre-Columbian Art and Archaeology*, by Samuel K. Lothrop, et. al., Harvard University Press, Cambridge, Mass. (1961), pp. 33, 34.

many readers to imply that these chariots had wheels. (This may or may not be the case.) Critics, unaware of any evidence of early use of the wheel in Mesoamerica, frequently use these references in the Book of Mormon in their criticism of the document.

Nephite and Lamanite chariots may or may not have had wheels: the argument does not hinge on whether they did or not but rather on whether people of the Book of Mormon knew about—and used— wheels. To support the premise that the Israelites referred to in the Book of Mormon came to the Americas, bringing with them knowledge of the wheel, we must look for examples of the wheel's use in ancient America.

Evidence

Until recently, scholars were of the opinion that the potter's wheel was not used anywhere in pre-Columbian America. But with a new find of a potter's wheel in the excavations of Pashash, Peru, scholars have reevaluated their views. Rotary tools, drill bits, and a spindle were also found there.[3]

Mesoamericans most certainly had knowledge of the wheel. Small wheeled objects, as seen in figure 6.1 through 6.4, would seem to verify this. In 1973, Stanley Boggs stated that sixty examples of wheeled objects had been found. Many more have been found since that publication appeared.[5]

Dr. Gordon F. Ekholm, of the Department of Anthropology at the American Museum of Natural History in New York, reports:

> During the winter of 1942, while I was making some excavations in Panuco and in the vicinity of Tampico, I found a certain number of small discs that I suspected of having been the wheels of rolling toys like those found by Dr. Stirling in Tres Zapotes and by Charnay in Popocatepetl. In the excavations of Panuco I felt most happy when my helper informed me of the finding of a complete toy with wheels just after having left the place myself and only a few meters from my excavation. This finding, together with the other known examples, convinced me that the Mexican Indians, before the conquest, had made small vehicles with wheels in the form of animals and therefore had some knowledge of the principle of the wheel.[6]

---

3. Terence Grieder, "Rotary Tools in Ancient Peru," *Archaeology*, Vol. 28, No. 3, July 1975, p. 178.

4. Only one-hundredth precent of Mesoamerican pre-Columbian sites have been excavated.

5. Stanley H. Boggs, "Salvadoran Varieties of Wheeled Figurines," *Institute of Maya Studies, Contributions to Mesoamerican Anthropology*, Publ. No. 1 (1973), p. 3.

6. Alfonso Caso, *Sobretiro de Cuadermos Americanos* (Mexico: Imprenta Mundial, 1946), p. 8.

Fig. 6.1. Spider monkey on wheels, from Veracruz. (Housed at the Milwaukee Public Museum.)

Fig. 6.2. Deer on wheels, from Veracruz. (Housed at the Milwaukee Public Museum.)

Fig. 6.3. Small wheeled vehicle, after Desire Charnay, *The Ancient Cities of the New World*, New York (1887).

Fig. 6.4. Wheeled animal, Tres Zapotes, Veracruz, Mexico. (On display at Museum of Jalapa, Veracruz.)

Scholars have found that five ways to attach wheels were used. This suggests that early Mesoamericans were not novices on the use of the axle.[7] If these small clay figures were modeled after larger, practical vehicles, we may never know exactly how they were used, since, in all likelihood, they were made of wood—and wood deteriorates with time.

Most of these figures portray dogs, although the style of some are so vague that it is difficult to determine the type of animal some figures were intended to portray. These figures have been found in most, but not all, parts of Mesoamerica, with the majority of examples found dating between A.D. 500 to 900. The earliest one found, in El Salvador, dates to approximately 100 B.C., well into Book of Mormon times.

It appears there was no utilitarian use of the wheel at the time of the Conquest. Perhaps there never was. Mesoamericans may have understood the principle of the wheel but decided not to use it for a reason, or reasons, unknown by researchers. Frazer's critical quote at the beginning of this chapter makes it evident that the natives were aware of the wheel as used by the Spanish, but that they chose not to use it. These are possible answers to the question of why the wheel was not used in a more utilitarian manner.

But perhaps the answer lies within priesthood organization since its members were usually the artisans chosen to portray objects of religious significance. It may be, therefore, that these people chose not to cast off the technology of the wheel, that they rejected the utilitarian use of the wheel because it was, for them, a sacred religious symbol. Frances Gibson, who lived among the Maya and studied their ways, found this to be true.

> One notes that the Mayas of Guatemala still walk and carry loads on their backs after more than four hundred years of exposure to wheels. I discussed this point not long ago with a modern Maya at Merida, Yucatan, and he informed me that the wheel was a symbol of the ancient sun god and as such it was a sacred symbol. This is obviously a possibility. One does not use the symbol of one's god in a disrespectful fashion.[8]

---

7. The most common method was an axle tube through holes in the legs of the terracotta animal, or horizontal holes in the body. See "Wheeled Toys in Mexico," by Gordon F. Ekholm, *American Antiquity*, 11, 4:222-8, (1946); "Wheels and Man," by Stephan F. de Borhegyi, *Archaeology*, 23 (Jan. 1970): 18-25; and Boggs, *op. cit.*
8. *Frances Gibson, The Seafarers: Pre-Columbian Voyages to America* (Philadelphia: Dorrance & Co., 1974), p. 63.

The wheel has long been a special design in the Americas—even the symbol of the sun, which is associated with deity and cyclical completion as depicted in the popular Aztec calendar which shows wheels within wheels. Few aspects of life, for the Aztecs and other Indian cultures, were not infused with religious meaning. Except for date, name, and place glyphs there is hardly an art form in Mesoamerica that does not have a religious connotation.

Not only did the wheel represent the sun, but the commonly portrayed dog, often carried on wheels, was also a symbol of the sun. With regard to this symbolism, the eminent archaeologist, J. Eric Thompson, stated:

> Both the dog and the jaguar are intimately associated with the underworld, the former because he led the sun and the dead to the underworld.[9]

In both the Old and New Worlds these figures were, more often than not, buried with the dead. The earthen tomb represented the underworld. Dr. Ekholm noted that this similarity appears even oceans apart when he wrote:

> Miniature clay vehicles in the form of animals have been found in Mesopotamia and [that] they are remarkably similar to those from Mexico.[10]

It was believed by peoples in both Old and New Worlds that the sun made its transit at night through the underworld. Thus we have the Mesoamerican dog, like the Egyptian dog Anubis, taking a role as a guide for the dead—giving the deceased a means of transportation through the underworld to the dawn of resurrection when the sun once more rises to the heavens. Thus a complete sacred cycle of death (the underworld) and rebirth (the rising sun) is portrayed in the combined symbol of dog and wheel.

This phenomenon alone would be reason enough to explain why the wheel was not used by the common people of Mesoamerica before the Conquest. However, since the wheel may have been used earlier, further research needs to be done to justify this hypothesis. We do know that, besides animals shown atop wheels, wheeled platforms have been found.[11] If the people knew how to construct a cart-like wheeled object,

---

9. J. Eric S. Thompson, "Maya Hieroglyphic Writing," *Carnegie Institution of Washington*, Publ. No. 589, pp. 172, 173.

10. Ekholm, "Wheeled Toys in Mexico," *op. cit.*, p. 227.

11. See "Animal Figurines on Wheels from Ancient Mexico," by Hasso von Winning, *Masterkey*, 24, (1950) 5:154-9.

they certainly knew they could employ the wheel in many other ways if they chose to do so.

What we need to ask is: Where did the concept of the wheel come from? Considering that the wheel was used in an identical way as a guide for the dead in both the Old and the New World there simply is no other explanation: We must look to the Old World for the source of these wheeled objects; the world Lehi and his family left to come to this land.

Conclusions

•Voyagers from the Old World to the Americas would have had knowledge of the principle of the wheel.

•The pottery wheel may have been used in Mesoamerica. A recent discovery proves that it was used in Peru where it was not previously thought to have existed.

•Terracotta-wheeled objects were buried with the dead in Mesoamerican as well as in Old World cultures.

•At least five methods of attaching an axle to a wheel were known in pre-Columbian America.

•Small wheeled carts have been discovered which were undoubtedly patterned after larger models.

•The wheel was a sacred emblem to the Indians and, for this reason, may have been considered "taboo" for utilitarian purposes.

Chapter 7

Lehi Tree of Life Stone

A certain account in the Book of Mormon, called Lehi's vision of the Tree of Life, gives a detailed description of a highly symbolic dream. The dream concerns the salvation of Lehi and his family and it depicts a prophetic warning along with the greatest gift of God available to mankind. This is illustrated through such symbols as the Tree of Life, white fruit, a rod of iron, and a straight path. Also symbolized are a filthy river, mists of darkness, and a spacious building filled with people who mock the attempts of others to reach the tree and partake of its fruit.

Many of these symbols appear in the "Tree of Life" stela, a massive volcanic stone found in Chiapas, Mexico, in 1939. Members and scholars of The Church of Jesus Christ of Latter-day Saints are well acquainted with the story of Lehi's dream. For many church members, it is a favorite passage of scripture. However, researchers who are not familiar with Lehi's account of the Tree of Life must start from point zero and try to piece together a scenario they know very little about.

Point

Lehi, a descendant of Manasseh, through Joseph, received a detailed vision of the Tree of Life, a common religious theme of the Old World from which he came. Portions of this vision are illustrated in stone in Izapa, Chiapas, Mexico.

References: 1 Nephi, chapters 8, 11, and 12.

Counterpoints

The "Tree of Life" stela, a carving found in Chiapas, Mexico, in the mid-sixties which has given a loud (but short-lived) heralding by Mormons as "proof" of Book of Mormon teachings, has been shown to have none of the connections to Mormonism once claimed for it.[1]

As we examine Dr. Jakeman's work we find that he has not actually translated any Book of Mormon name from "Stela 5," but he has only "symbolically" interpreted some elements on the stone.[2]

As to the "jawbone" name glyph, this is highly conjectural. Is it a personal name glyph? If so, should only the jaw portion of the crocodile emblem be singled out to signify the name? Dr. Jakeman himself stated that the crocodile symbol may signify the earth, the first day of the ancient religious calendar, or several characters in Mesoamerican tradition. Why, then, should another meaning be sought?[3]

Commentary

Father Lehi, a prophet of God in both Jerusalem and the western hemisphere [circa 600 B.C.], had a remarkable vision, or dream, concerning the Tree of Life which merits our attention. From the viewpoint of the discussion in this book, passages in the Book of Mormon that relate to this incident are some of the most significant verses in the entire book because of their many correlations with evidence of an archaeological nature in the New World.

To visualize the scene as Lehi saw it, we must examine each part of his dream in a subjective manner. Some of the more pertinent parts of his vision are listed below along with an interpretation of each symbol as given to the prophet Nephi.

LEHI'S VISION OF THE TREE OF LIFE

Lehi's Vision	Nephi's Interpretation
Tree of Life—the main object of the vision, the fruit of which is very desirable. (1 Nephi 8:10-12; 11:8)	*Love of God*—a means of obtaining eternal life for those who partake of the fruit of the Tree of Life. (1 Nephi 11:25)
River of Water—running near the tree. (1 Nephi 8:13-14, 32)	*Hell*—representing the gulf which separates the wicked from the Tree of Life. (1 Nephi 12:16)
Rod of Iron—extending along the bank of the river which leads to the tree. (1 Nephi 8:19-20, 24, 30)	

---

1. Latayne Colvett Scott, *The Mormon Mirage* (Grand Rapids, Michigan: Zondervan Publishing House, 1980), second printing, pp. 81, 82.

2. Jerald and Sandra Tanner, *Archaeology and the Book of Mormon* (Salt Lake City: Modern Microfilm Co., 1969), p. 37.

3. Hal Hougey, "The Truth About the 'Lehi Tree-of-Life' Stone," a pamphlet, Pacific Publishing Co., Concord, California (1963), p. 13.

Lehi's Vision (cont.)	Nephi's Interpretation (cont.)
Great and Spacious Building—as though it were in the air, full of people dressed in fine attire, mocking those partaking of the fruit of the tree. (1 Nephi 8:26-27, 31, 33)	*Word of God*—one who holds onto the iron rod, or word of God, cannot go astray in the world or fall into the murky depths of hell. (1 Nephi 11:25)
	The Pride of the World—those of the materialistic world who scorn those who seek after righteousness: a great building that will eventually be destroyed. (1 Nephi 12:18)

A unique stone monument was discovered in 1939 (not in the sixties as cited by Scott above). It is now known as Stela 5, Izapa, Chiapas, Mexico. In 1941, the stela was examined by members of the Smithsonian Institution and the National Geographic Society: the stela has been of special interest to LDS scholars for the past thirty-odd years. Not only does this bas-relief contain the major elements of design referred to in Lehi's dream, but it portrays many other features relevant to "Tree of Life" themes in the Old World. Figure 7.1 presents arrowed information on these features.

LDS archaeologists are not in total agreement with regard to the interpretation of this complex stela. They all admit, however, that there is a strong parallel between elements portrayed on the stela and similar themes found in the Old World. Therefore, in the Mormon community, there is no singular opinion regarding this stela. As discussed earlier, archaeological interpretations are theories—not Church doctrine.

Evidence

Ancient Sources Support Lehi's Vision

Inscribed tablets of gold that contain Orphic poetry have been found in the Old World as recently as 1976. Orphism, a Greek religious movement, was popular in the sixth century B.C., Lehi's lifetime. Scholars have suggested an Egyptian origin for the Orphic texts. However, they may not be "Orphic" at all since this name has been given to them by modern scholars.[4]

These texts are of religious significance: they evolve around the theme of the fate of the soul in the spirit world. The tablets describe

---

4. See Gunther Zuntz, *Persephone*, Oxford: Clarendon Press (1971), p. 326; Pseudo-Plato, *Axiochos*, p. 371a; W. K. C. Guthrie, *Orpheus and Greek Religion* (New York: W. W. Norton & Co., 1966); and "The Book of Mormon as an Ancient Book," by Wilfred Griggs in *Book of Mormon Authorship: New Light on Ancient Origins*, Noel B. Reynolds, Editor, BYU, Provo (1982), pp. 75-101.

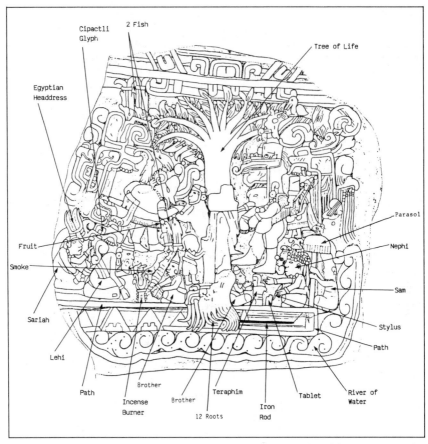

Fig. 7.1. Tree of Life, Stela 5, Izapa, Chiapas, Mexico. Reproduced from *Izapa Sculpture*, New World Archaeological Foundation (1976), p. 165, courtesy of author, V. Garth Norman. (Arrowed information supplied by Diane E. Wirth.)

many of the elements in the scene portrayed on Stela 5, and—more particularly—Lehi's vision of the Tree of Life as found in the Book of Mormon. Languages similar to the Orphic texts have also been found on a papyrus from Egypt, and even earlier Egyptian funerary texts contain the same theme of the Tree of Life.[5]

These ancient texts give strong evidence that the vision of Lehi, as recounted in the Book of Mormon, was not a figment of Joseph Smith's imagination. The symbolism in this prophecy was apparently given by God on several occasions to his holy prophets. It is also

---

5. Griggs, *ibid.*

significant that many of these Orphic texts were inscribed on metal tablets as was the Book of Mormon.

A Close-up of Stela 5

This volcanic stone monument, which stands eight feet high and is six feet wide, portrays a group of people seated at the base of a tree. In the background are many complex designs. The first seated figure, at the left of the tree, is a woman who wears a tall-horned and feathered headdress not unlike that worn by Hathor, a mother-goddess figure in Egypt. A likely prototype for this Mesoamerican mother figure would be Sariah, wife of the prophet Lehi and matriarch of her lineage.

In front of the woman sits a bearded old man wearing a pointed cap or turban typical of those worn by Semitic high priests in the Near East during the time period we are concerned with. The pointed cap, worn by the elderly man and one other figure on Stela 5, is significant in light of Old World traditions in which hats of this type were worn. According to J. Forlong, who has made a study of ancient cultures, the "cone hat" was frequently worn by priests and kings: it was meant to identify the sect and rank (of nobility) of the wearer.[6] The famous Black Obelisk at the British Museum in London, of Shalmaneser III, King of Assyria, portrays King Jehu of Israel, kneeling before his capture, and Jehu wears the typical pointed cap.[7] The pointed cap was also popular in Mesoamerica where it was worn only by priests.[8]

Above the old man's head is a name glyph which is a use customary in Mesoamerican art. It is this name glyph that identifies our bearded elder as Lehi.

Dr. Wells Jakeman recognized this design as the *Cipactli* glyph, or crocodile glyph.[9] This glyph is unusual in that it represents an abbreviated crocodile head portraying the upper jaw. As we will see, this glyph was of great significance in Mesoamerican art and meaningful to us by its use in relation to the Old World. The Hebrew word for upper jaw means "Lehee" or Lehi. The incident wherein Samson slays the Philistines with a jawbone is related in Judges 15:9 and 15:15.

---

6. J. G. R. Forlong, *Rivers of Life*, London (1883).

7. See *Story of the Bible*, Reader's Digest, Pleasantville, New York (1962), p. 81.

8. Alfred M. Tozzer, "Landa's Relacion de las Cosas de Yucatan: A Translation. *Papers of the Peabody Museum of Archaeology and Ethnology, Harvard University*, Vol. 18. Cambridge (1941), p. 153, n. 764.

9. M. Wells Jakeman "Stela 5, Izapa, as 'The Lehi Tree-of-Life Stone,' " *The Tree of Life in Ancient America*, Ross T. Christensen, Editor, BYU.

This historic event, in Judah, gives the site the name of Lehi as recorded in these Biblical passages in the book of Judges.

There is an obvious correlation between the Mesoamerican jaw glyph and the Hebrew word for jaw. To the layman, Mayan and Aztec glyphs may appear to be strange indeed. In many cases, these glyphs have more than one meaning; this is certainly true of the crocodile, or "Cipactli," glyph. Symbolic representations are a common and expected feature of pre-Columbian art. A study of these various interpretations strengthens the hypothesis that the Cipactli glyph does represent Lehi who was not only a seer, but who was considered the father of his lineage who came to the promised land.

The Cipactli glyph was used in Mesoamerica as a calendrical sign as well as a name glyph to identify the name of the person by whom the glyph was placed. Day and month names and their ideographic patrons are usually considered to have some historical or mythological background. Nahua (Mexican) mythology has it that there were two original creators, one male, the other female. Throughout Mesoamerica these creators were given different names, but what is interesting here is that the creative deities ruled over the day Cipactli.[10]

J. Eric Thompson explains that creation gods are derived from ancestral gods, usually Father-Mother pairs.[11] In Mesoamerica it was not unusual for the Mesoamericans to deify ancestors or famous historical persons. In fact a descendant of Nephi, also named Nephi, was declared by some to be a god (Helaman 9:40, 41). The elder couple portrayed on Stela 5 fall into this category of deified historical personages. Thus it is the opinion of many LDS scholars that the couple at the left of the tree on Stela 5 represent Lehi and Sariah, the two forebearers of their race.

Eduard Seler, of the University of Berlin, was a famed professor of linguistics, ethnography, and archaeology. In his commentary on the *Codex Borgia* he discussed the Cipactli figure portrayed. He observed that the jewels issuing from the hands of this personage portrayed as sitting in an attitude of delivering a child, denote the offspring of Cipactli.[12] The portrayal of Cipactli as a father figure in Mesoamerican art is in agreement with our knowledge of Lehi as the

---

10. J. Eric Thompson, *Maya History and Religion*, (Norman: University of Oklahoma Press, 1976), pp. 200-201.

11. *Ibid.*, pp. 201-203.

12. Eduard Seler, *Codex Vaticanus*, Vol. 2, London (1902-1903), p. 247.

forefather of his ruling family in Mesoamerica according to the Book of Mormon.

Seler further stated that "Cipactli"—the sign of a crocodilian upper jaw—was a major sign used to designate one who was a diviner, or prophet.[13] Father Lehi was a prophet. The evidence clearly supports the hypothesis that the original Cipactli glyph in Mesoamerica refers to none other than Lehi, prophet and progenitor of the Nephite/Lamanite people.

Across from Lehi, our father figure, we see two figures seated on either side of the tree. Because they are seated with their backs to the tree, Dr. Jakeman theorizes that these two persons may represent the two rebellious sons of Lehi, Laman and Lemuel. According to the Book of Mormon, Laman and Lemuel did not partake of the fruit of the tree in Lehi's dream. Their posture may symbolize their negative attitude and unworthiness (1 Nephi 8:17, 18).

Although these two personages may be Laman and Lemuel, as identified by Jakeman, it is possible that they represent two other family members. The person facing Lehi wears a pointed cap designating him a priest,[14] as was Lehi. Likely candidates for the two men thus portrayed would be Nephi's brothers, Sam and Joseph, who were worthy priesthood holders.

Next to the personage seated at the right of the tree is a small figure. According to scholars, this may be either a child or an ancestral image. The ancient Hebrews had images in their households called "teraphim" which, as a rule, were not worshipped but kept as a remembrance of their ancestors.[15]

Like the ancient Hebrews, Mesoamericans kept ancestral images in their household. Comments published along with the *Codex Vaticanus* support this conjecture:

> They put great stock in family descent, and when they make offerings, they would say, "I am of such and such a lineage." They worshipped and sacrificed to the first founder, calling him "the heart of the people," and they kept him, in the form of an idol, in a secure place, offering him gold and precious stones.[16]

---

13. Eduard Seler, *The Tonalamatl of the Aubin Collection*, Berlin and London (1900), p. 9.

14 Alfred M. Tozzer, "Landa's Relacion de las Cosas de Yucatan: a Translation," *Papers of the Peabody Museum of Archaeology and Ethnology, Harvard University*, Vol. 18, Cambridge (1941), p. 153, footnote 764.

15. M. Wells Jakeman, "Stela 5, etc.," *op. cit.*

16. *Codex Vaticanus Latinus* 3788 (Codex Rios). In Vol. 3, p. 5 of Antiguedades de Mexico, basadas en la recopilacion de Lord Kingsborough. 4 Vols. Mexico City: secretaria de Hacienda y Credito Publico (1964).

The Izapa carving was made hundreds of years after Lehi's death. If this is a Mesoamerican teraph, which is portrayed on Stela 5, it may represent Lehi himself since he was regarded as the ancestor of his people.

To the right of the tree a man holding a stylus is seen. He is represented as listening to the narrative of the old man and prepared to make a record of the account. A plate, or tablet, can be seen directly under the stylus, or engraving, instrument. With an outstretched hand this scribe, identified as Nephi, listens and records the vision of his father, Lehi.

Nephi was greatly loved by members of his family. The Book of Mormon tells us he was close to the Lord, gave his family spiritual guidance and was the record keeper of their early history (1 Nephi 1:1-3). For this reason he was depicted as a ruler, indicated by the parasol held over this scribe's head. Nephi became the leader of his people after his father's death. Using an umbrella in this manner to designate their ruler was also a custom practiced among the ancient people of the Near East.[17]

Other Elements

The Tree of Life is a theme that runs like a gold thread throughout Mesoamerican mythology. The sacred tree of the Maya stood for a tree of abundance and/or life. Corresponding to the Tree of Life in the garden of Eden, this Mesoamerican tree was set up at the time of the creation, at the center of the world. In the underworld, the tree served as a means for the dead to reach the various layers of the heavens. Thompson gives us a description of the many symbolic facets of this sacred tree:

> A giant ceiba tree, the sacred tree of the Maya, the *yaxche*, "first" or "green" tree, stands in the exact center of the earth. Its roots penetrate the underworld; its trunk and branches pierce the various layers of the skies. Some Maya groups hold that by its roots their ancestors ascended into the world, and by its trunk and branches the dead climb to the highest sky.[18]

This scenario is portrayed in Stela 5 as well. The roots of the tree twist their way into the womb of the underworld while its branches

---

17. Garth Norman, *Izapa Sculpture*, New World Archaeological Foundation, No. 30, Part 2, BYU, Provo, Utah (1976), p. 172.

18. Thompson, *Maya History and Religion, op. cit.*, p. 195. See also Norman, *op. cit.*, pp. 201-2.

thrust their way up through the heavens, represented as a celestial skyband. Consequently the interpretation of this stela deals strongly with the life, death, and resurrection of man.[19] This is also the theme of 1 Nephi, chapters 8 and 11.

The tree itself has several symbolic messages. Of particular significance are the roots and their relation to lineages. It is well-known that the "genealogical tree" originated in the Old World. Joseph's blessing in Genesis 49:22 is an example of the tree's early symbolism among the Hebrews as related in the Old Testament. In the New World, the Tzotzils of Chiapas, Mexico, believed their ancestors came from the roots of the ceiba tree,[20] and the Xiu family of the Mani of the Yucatan give us an interesting portrayal of this family's lineage sprouting from the loins of a man (see figure 12.1).

These symbolic messages lead us back to the roots portrayed on Stela 5. Although this part of the stone is somewhat weathered, there appear to be either twelve or thirteen roots to the tree. It would not be out of line here to suggest that the roots may correspond to the twelve tribes of Israel; if thirteen, Joseph's two sons, Ephraim and Manasseh, would account for the thirteenth root, or tribe.[21]

The commentary footnote in the work by Recinos and Goetz regarding the thirteen clans mentioned in *The Annals of the Cakchiquels*, refers to another genealogical account recorded by the Quiche Maya:

> The Popol Vuh also states that there were thirteen branches of the people who came from the East.[22]

Thirteen clans figure prominently in both Quiche and Cakchiquel ancestral histories; both claim they came from across the sea, from the direction of the rising sun, as did Lehi and his people.

If we follow the smoke from the incense burner in front of Lehi, in this fascinating story in stone, we see that two fish are partaking of the fruit of the Tree of Life. They appear to rise upward. The two fish are then portrayed hanging over the old woman and man from

---

19. See Norman, *ibid.*, pp. 195, 201-2.

20. See Maya Hieroglyphic Writing," by J. Eric S. Thompson, *Carnegie Institute of Washington*, Publication 589, Washington, D.C. (1950), p. 71.

21. See Norman, *op. cit.*, pp. 197, 207, and 208.

22. *Annals of the Cakchiquels*, translated from the Cakchiquel Maya by Adrian Recinos and Delia Goetz, University of Oklahoma, Norman (1974), p. 48, footnote 26.

what is referred to as a "skyband." I believe that these fish symbolically represent Lehi and Sariah in a celestial state.

There are many astronomical and astrological signs on this stela.
In Old World mythology, two fish stood for the sign of Pisces. Since
these fish are portrayed as a sign in the heavens, it is plausible to con-
clude that they represent this sign of the zodiac.

A possible interpretation for the two fish hanging from the celestial band may coincide with the findings of Oral E. Scott in his work
on ancient cosmologies. With reference to the sign of the two fish,
Scott states:

> An old interpretation of the symbolism is that the two fishes, joined together
> by a ribbon, representing the heavenly marriage of true mates. This exalted
> state, however, has been reached only after . . . disobedience to Divine law,
> has been overcome. . . . In Pisces they are united by the bond of true love,
> no longer separated but parts of a whole, joined together by God, or Divine
> Law, having learned that this is the fruit of the Tree of Life.[23]

Certain points of interest are contained in this symbolic lore of
the past. First, we have two symbolic fish traveling through life as
a pair. Second, we note that the union of the fish, or the "heavenly
marriage of true mates," brings to them an awareness that they have
earned the fruit of the Tree of Life. As in the Book of Mormon account,
the fruit of the tree, which they earn, is a gift of the love of God to
the righteous. The concept of the marriage vow being consummated
by "Divine Law" is a beautiful one, and, because this information
comes to us from an ancient source, it should be considered as a possible interpretation of the two fish on this remarkable stela.

When the elements of the Tree of Life theme in the Americas
are viewed, many factors need to be considered. Studies of ancient
Tree of Life texts in the Old World are just now becoming significant
in scholarly circles and they join together, in content, with the account
of Lehi's vision of the Tree of Life as related in the Book of Mormon.

Conclusions

•A stela, found in Mesoamerica well after Joseph Smith's time,
portrays most of othe basic elements of Lehi's vision of the Tree of
Life as related in the Book of Mormon.

•Old World texts refer to similar scenes of the Tree of Life scenario.

---

23. Oral E. Scott, *The Stars in Myth and Fact* (Caldwell, Idaho: Caxton Printers, Ltd., 1942), pp. 136, 137.

•Lehi is portrayed on Stela 5 as a priest and father of his race. His name appears over his head in glyph form.

•Mesoamerican glyphs frequently have more than one symbolic meaning, as does the Cipactli (Lehi) glyph over the bearded elder in this story in stone.

•The teraphim may represent Lehi: ancestral statues of this type were a tradition in both the Old and New Worlds.

•A scribe of royal lineage is portrayed as he records the words of the old man. He is identified as Nephi, the first author of the Book of Mormon.

•The Tree of Life theme is one of life, death, and resurrection in both the Old and New Worlds.

•The roots of the tree refer to the lineage of the people, more particularly to the House of Israel.

•The two fish hanging from the heavens may represent Lehi and Sariah who have achieved their eternal objective after having partaken of the fruit of the Tree of Life.

Chapter 8

Ancient American Scripts and Reformed Egyptian

Reformed Egyptian, the script used in the Book of Mormon, was unheard of in 1830 when the book was published. However, there are scholars today who are aware of various styles of reformed Egyptian.

Point

The historians who wrote the Book of Mormon on the American continent used a written language called "reformed Egyptian." *Reference:* Moroni 9:32-33.

Counterpoints

Many Mormons see similarities between Mayan hieroglyphics and the reformed Egyptian scribbles of Joseph Smith (which Charles Shook called "deformed English"). Most archaeologists see few such similarities.[1]

In 600 B.C., and in the holy city of Jerusalem, to render "the learning of the Jews" into the decadent and clumsy Egyptian would have been utterly unthinkable.[2]

Commentary

Until recently, the study of New World inscriptions has been greatly neglected. In fact, in Joseph Smith's time, pre-Columbian Indians were considered to have been illiterate. Even today there is the unresolved question of whether or not the ancient inhabitants of the Americas had a written script. Most archaeologists speak solely of the hieroglyphic picture writing used by the Maya, shown in figure 8.1, and, in figure 8.2, the knotted string quipu used by the Incas of

---

1. Latayne Colvet Scott, *The Mormon Mirage* (Grand Rapids, Michigan: Zondervan Publishing House, 2d printing, 1980), p. 82.
2. Gordon H. Fraser, *What Does the Book of Mormon Teach?* (Chicago: Moody Press, 1964), p. 31.

Fig. 8.1. Typical Maya hieroglyphs from the Temple of Inscriptions at Palenque, Chiapas, Mexico.

Peru. Anything further in the way of a written language is questioned by most scholars.

However, ancient inscriptions are being discovered and studied by epigraphists. As a result, we are beginning to see a new and different picture of early America than has been portrayed in our history books. The aforementioned inscribed wall at Chatata, Tennessee, is a prime example of a script found in the Americas which has its roots in the Old World.

Because many of these newly found scripts have an affinity with Old World languages, the law of deduction gives us several choices to explain inscriptions found in the Americas. Either they were planted as forgeries, they were authentic ancient scripts brought to the Americas in modern days, or they were written in pre-Columbian times by races whose people originally came from the Old World. As we will see, there are numerous ancient inscriptions beginning to be recognized as genuine as they are validated by scholars.

Although various styles of writing have been found in the Americas, LDS scholars do not claim any of them as "proof" of the Book of Mormon. In fact, aside from Mayan hieroglyphs, few of these means of a communicating language are alike. For example, in North America, the writings vary greatly. In Mesoamerica, where the Book of Mormon accounts took place, archaeologists are aware of at least thirteen glyphic writing systems: even more may yet be found.[3]

Fig. 8.2. The ancient Peruvian quipu. This device was used to keep records, and to some extent was used as a substitute for the written word. The color indicated the subject dealt with on the knots, and the knots, made with differing numbers of turns of the cord, are decimals varying from one to ten. As the knots descend, the number increases up into the thousands.

3. See Michael D. Coe, "Early Steps in the Evolution of Maya Writing," in H. B. Nicholson, ed., *Origins of Religious Art and Iconography in Preclassic Mesoamerica*, Los Angeles: UCLA Latin American Center and Ethnic Arts Council of Los Angeles (1976), pp. 110ff. Olmec scripts were not included in Coe's list, which would increase his number by at least two.

What many of these early American scripts do tell us is that they had their roots in Old World scripts; that they could not possibly have sprung up out of the blue. Transoceanic voyages must be considered. Some of these scripts will be looked at and the concept of a reformed Egyptian script examined—the style the Book of Mormon authors claimed they used.

Evidence

Bat Creek Inscription

Of particular note is the Bat Creek Stone, shown in figure 8.3. This stone was excavated during the Smithsonian Mound Exploration Program under the direction of Professor Cyrus Thomas, in 1885, in Loudon County, Tennessee.

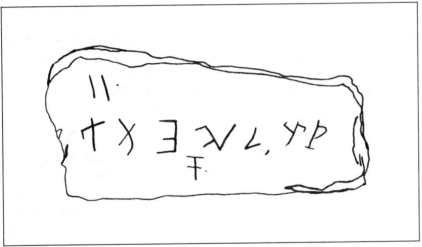

Fig. 8.3. Bat Creek inscription. Adapted from *Riddles in History* by Cyrus A. Gordon. Copyright © 1974 by Cyrus A. Gordon. (Used by permission of Crown Publishers, Inc.)

What makes this story interesting is that the Smithsonian, in its official report dated 1894, unknowingly published a photograph of the object upside down. Joseph Mahan Jr., Director of Education and Research at the Columbus (Georgia) Museum of Arts and Crafts, noticed that something was amiss with the positioning of the photograph. When it is turned right side up, we have a clear, archaic Hebrew phrase (which can be read as LYHWD) reading "For the Land of Judah." The well-known Dr. Cyrus H. Gordon, a scholar of ancient languages, was responsible for the interpretation. He claims that this discovery implies Middle East contact with the New World of around A.D. 100 which was one of several periods during which Jewish persecution by the Romans took place.

Dr. Gordon speaks very firmly about his translation of this artifact.

> The Bat Creek inscription inscribed in Roman antiquity is not a souvenir imported from the Old World after 1492 to gratify some Cherokee chief's love of East Mediterranean archaeology—a love so great that he took the inscribed stone with him for eternity in the next life. The script was not even deciphered until the nineteenth century. Trying to explain away the Bat Creek evidence as anything other than American contact with Palestine around the second century A.D. can only amount to obscurantism that no sensible scholar or layman should elect. The Atlantic was crossed long before the Vikings, by different peoples during different centuries.[4]

There is no implication here that this stone has anything to do with the Book of Mormon in a direct manner. What it does show, however, is the possibility that Israelites came to America in pre-Columbian times, even though this voyage was made at a later date than voyages referred to in the Book of Mormon.

Brazilian Inscriptions

Professor Marcel F. Homet, archaeologist, explorer, professor of classic Arabic, and writer of some renown traveled through the more remote regions of Brazil. He is convinced that white races of high intellect came to South America in ancient times. At the Pedra Pintada on the Brazilian plains, he found an egg-shaped stone covered with inscriptions. He is of the opinion that these engravings have an ancient Mediterranean influence.[5]

Professor Homet's discoveries are just a few of hundreds of similar characters found carved on cliffs and boulders throughout South America. Some scholars say that these inscriptions closely resemble ancient Mediterranean and North African languages. Therefore, we can surmise that many of the ancient peoples in this area were also from the Old World. In other words, not all pre-Columbian

---

4. Cyrus H. Gordon, *Before Columbus: Links Between the Old World and Ancient America* (New York: Crown, 1971), p. 187. See also *Riddles in History*, by Cyrus H. Gordon (New York: Crown, 1974), pp. 145-146.
5. Marcel F. Homet, *Sons of the Sun*, Neville Spearman, London (1963), (translated from the German edition by Elizabeth R. Hapgood).

inhabitants came by way of the Bering Strait, and thus had their roots in Asia, as has hitherto been accepted as a historical fact.

Phoenician Inscriptions

What is considered to be one of the most important finds in South America is referred to as the Paraiba Text, seen in figure 8.4. It contains a Phoenician inscription that was found in 1872 at Pouso Alto near Paraiba, Brazil. For years this script remained unpublished and was unnoticed by scholars. When Professor Jules Piccus became aware of the inscription, he sent a copy of the text to Cyrus H. Gordon of the Department of Mediterranean Studies at Brandeis University in Massachusetts.[6]

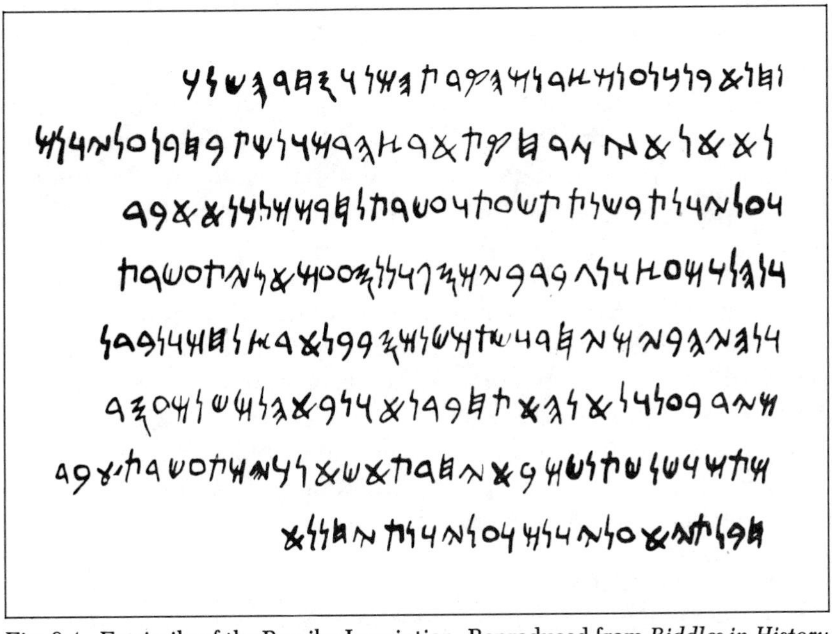

Fig. 8.4. Facsimile of the Paraiba Inscription. Reproduced from *Riddles in History* by Cyrus H. Gordon (by permission of Crown Publishers, Inc.)

There are archaeologists who support Dr. Gordon's findings, and there are those who do not. Actually, there are very few archaeological finds made by laymen that are not controversial. We merely present the findings and look forward to further study and results.

---

6. Gordon, *Riddles in History, op. cit.*, chapter III.

Using the historical names contained within the text as a guide, it was Dr. Gordon's expert opinion that this group of mariners left Canaan in 534 B.C., arriving in Brazil in 531 B.C. Whether the voyage was accidental or planned cannot be determined; but it is known that most ancient voyages were intentional and made along known routes, and this trip could have been made because of a need for Brazil's minerals, particularly iron. Ezekiel 27 gives us a vivid description of Phoenician navigation in the sixth century B.C., and historians acknowledge that the Phoenicians were the finest seafarers of their time.

Inscriptions from Mexico

Mexico's inscriptions deserve more consideration, with regard to Book of Mormon geography, than do other areas because of its geographical location.

Worth discussing are inscriptions from one of the earliest cultures of the New World, the Olmec. These ancient people lived during the time period corresponding to the Jaredite nation and the beginning of the Nephite and Lamanite civilizations referred to in the Book of Mormon.

In 1955, the Drucker-Heizer expedition found, at La Venta, sixteen figurines of jade and serpentine.[7] Each figurine seems to have been sculpted after a particular dignitary and was possibly intended to show different races since various colors of stone were used. Among these figures stood six celts, some bearing glyphs as in figure 8.5. To date, archaeologists have not been able to completely decipher the Olmec script, but they are of the opinion that this script was a forerunner of that used by the ancient Maya.

Mayan and Egyptian Hieroglyphs

Although Egyptian hieroglyphics and Mayan glyphs are not the same writing system, they do have things in common that are unique. According to Linda Van Blerkom, who studied these two systems of writing, Mayan glyphs are used in the same six ways Egyptian glyphs are used. They would include: (1) the primary pictograph; (2) associate pictures; (3) abstract signs; (4) semantic indicators; (5) phonetic signs; and (6) phonetic clarifying complements. All in all, Egyptian

---

7. Philip Drucker, et al., "Excavations at La Venta, Tabasco," *Bureau of American Ethnology*, Bulletin 170, Washington (1959).

hieroglyphics and Mayan glyphs are both "word-syllabic, utilizing some ideographs (word-signs) and some phonetic signs."[8]

Scholars have had more time to study Egyptian scripts than they have had to study the Mayan. Therefore they are more adept in trans-lating Egyptian texts than they are in translating the Mayan. To date, most of the progress made in translating the Mayan glyphs has been with names, dates, and places, apparently having to do with everyday affairs of the ruling classes. The work of translation is slow. Nobody is predicting a sudden understanding of Mayan glyphs. But, as time progresses, so does our understanding of the records of their history that the Maya left behind.

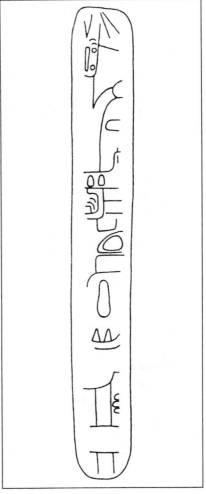

Roller Stamps

A form of personal identification in Mesopotamia of the Old World was the cylinder seal. This small, cylindrical clay object was engraved with either writing or pictures. When it was rolled over a surface of wax or soft clay, the cylindrical object left an image in panorama form. These seals could also be inked and rolled on parchment or skin. Many such seals or stamps have been found in Preclassic Mesoamerican irrigation ditches, on the sandy banks of rivers washed up by the current, and in archaeological excavations. Most of them are

Fig. 8.5. Celt from La Venta Offering. From "An Olmec Figure at Dumbarton Oaks," by Elizabeth P. Benson, Dumbarton Oaks, Washington, D.C. (1971), Figure 38, p. 28.

---

8. Linda Miller Van Blerkom, "A Comparison of Maya and Egyptian Hieroglyphs," *Katunob*, Dept. of Anthropology, University of Colorado, Boulder (August 1979):1-8.

engraved with designs that were used to decorate the skin, but of special significance to archaeologists are those with inscriptions.

Two clay roller stamps from early cultures in Mexico bear inscriptions with characters similar to the characters from the Anthon Transcript drawn from a plate of the Book of Mormon.[9] The first cylindrical stamp was found at La Venta, and although only a portion of it remains, there are Anthon Transcript equivalents for all of the visible characters on this stamp.[10]

An even more interesting linear script from the era before Christ, and one which corresponds to Book of Mormon times, comes from Tlatilco in the Valley of Mexico (figure 8.6). Dr. Kelley, who investigated this artifact, declares it to be a "hitherto unknown writing system."[11] (This roller stamp is housed in the Milwaukee Public Museum.)

All but two of the symbols on the Tlatilco stamp have an identifiable counterpart with the Anthon Transcript's characters (figure 8.7). Grouping of like characters also supports the theory that the Tlatilco stamp is a bonafide example of the type of script represented in Joseph Smith's sample of reformed Egyptian.[12] The striking similarities between the Anthon Transcript and these roller stamps is unique and worthy of note.

Reformed Egyptian

In Mesoamerica, those who were educated in the art of writing were members of the priesthood; even then, these languages were kept secret within each of the private religious organizations. This was especially true of Nephite historians. Mormon wrote that "none other people knoweth our language" (Mormon 9:34).

The Book of Mormon makes it clear that each person chosen to record prophetic and historic writings of their people was trained to write a unique script. It was not a "universal language," as many critics

9. This transcript has been coined the "Anthon Transcript," named after Professor Charles Anthon who gave his opinion of the characters. See statement from Charles Anthon to the Rev. T. W. Coit, 3 Apr. 1841, quoted in John A. Clark, *Gleanings By The Way* (Philadelphia: W. J. and J. K. Simon, 1842), pp. 232-38.

10. See "La Venta, Tabasco: A Study of Olmec Ceramics and Art," by Philip Drucker, *BAE Bulletin 153*, Smithsonian Institution: Washington (1952), Figure 43; "The 'Anthon Transcript' and Two Mesoamerican Cylinder Seals," by Carl Hugh Jones, *Newsletter and Proceedings of the SEHA*, No. 122, Sept. 1970, Provo, Utah.

11. David H. Kelley, "A Cylinder Seal From Tlatilco," *American Antiquity*, Vol. 31, No. 5, Part 1 (July). Society for American Archaeology (1966).

12. Jones, *op. cit.*, p. 7.

Fig. 8.6. Roller stamp from Tlatilco, Mexico, after photograph, *American Antiquity*, Vol. 31, No. 5, Part I (July 1966).

are quick to surmise,[13] but rather like the secret language similar to many used by priests in the Americas. Daniel Brinton wrote of this esoteric language as follows:

> To add to their self-importance they pretended to converse in a tongue different from that used in ordinary life, and the chants containing the prayers and legends were often in this esoteric dialect.[14]

It is highly possible that these secret languages were not pretense, but a reality, for it was known that only members of the priesthood could interpret their script: this was particularly true of the Maya. When priesthood and high government officials were assassinated by would-be usurpers of their theocratic government, there was no longer anyone to translate these symbols. By the time the Spanish arrived in 1519, no member of the priesthood could be found who was able to translate the glyphs.

King Benjamin, in Mosiah 1:4, explains that Lehi was taught in the language of the Egyptians and could therefore write these engravings. Lehi taught his children who taught their children, and so on to King Benjamin's time (circa 130 B.C.]. Yet Lehi and his descendants did not write in pure Egyptian nor in pure Hebrew: they wrote in an altered mixture of both. Moroni, the last prophet and the last author of the Book of Mormon identifies the characters of the script he and his forefathers used as "reformed Egyptian, being handed down

---

13. Martin Thomas Lamb, *The Golden Bible; or, the Book of Mormon. Is It From God?* (New York: Ward & Drummond, 1887), p. 159.
14. Daniel Brinton, *Myths of the New World*, Rudolf Steiner Publications (1976 edition of 1868 original), p. 302.

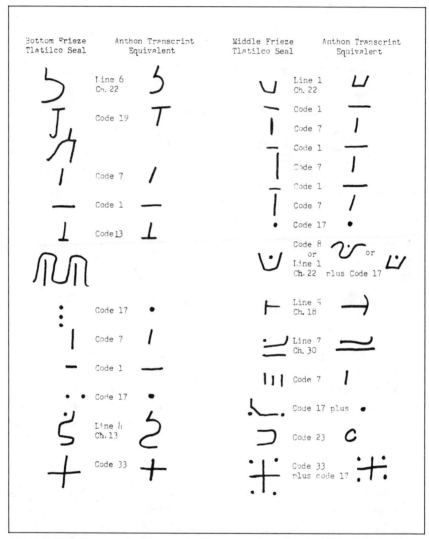

Fig. 8.7. Markings on the inscribed roller stamp found at Tlatilco, Valley of Mexico, and Anthon Transcript equivalents. (After "The 'Anthon Transcript' and Two Mesoamerican Cylinder Seals," by Carl Hugh Jones, SEHA Newsletter and Proceedings, BYU, Provo, No. 122, Fig. 8. See also updated article on Anthon Transcript in SEHA Newsletter 145, August 1980.)

and altered by us, according to our manner of speech" (Mormon 9:32). And Nephi wrote, "Yea, I make a record in the language of my father, which consists of the learning of the Jews and the language of the Egyptians" (1 Nephi 1:2).

As can be seen, the unknown written language of "reformed Egyptian" has been, and still is, a frequent target for critics of the Book of Mormon, because no such Egyptian cursive writing had been heard of when the Book of Mormon was made public. However, since Joseph Smith's proclamation, the word "Demotic" has come into general use. Demotic is an abbreviated style of Egyptian cursive writing (see figure 8.8). In fact, it has been found that this particular style of writing was widely used during the period in which the Book of Mormon commenced—approximately 600 B.C.

The Demotic text is inscribed on the historical Rosetta Stone. Discovered in 1799 when Napoleon invaded Egypt, the famed Rosetta Stone proved to be the key to unlocking the secrets of Egyptian hieroglyphics. The inscription, written in triplicate, gives honor to the Pharaoh Ptolemy V Epiphanes (196 B.C.) in two languages (Egyptian and Greek), but in three scripts (Hieroglyphic and Demotic Egyptian,

Fig. 8.8. A portion of Psalm 20:2-6. Hebrew prose in Aramaic language, written in Egyptian demotic script. (See "Bible's Psalm 20 Adapted for Pagan Use," *Biblical Archaeology Review*, Jan./Feb. 1985, Vol. XI, No. 1, p. 20, for complete photograph of this second century B.C. papyrus.)

and Greek). Although Jean-Francois Champollion supplied his brilliant key to the decipherment of hieroglyphic script in a letter dated 27 September 1822 (in French), to M. Dacier, it was not until 1837 that the grammar worked out from the Rosetta Stone was first published in English—after the publication of the Book of Mormon. (The Rosetta Stone is now housed in the British Museum.)

We know of a peculiar script today that was developed from the Demotic and is still largely undeciphered Egyptian script. This unusual Meroitic script could also be termed "reformed Egyptian." The Meroitic, Hieratic, and Demotic styles of writing are all modifications of the original Egyptian hieroglyphic picture writing: in this sense they constitute a reformed style of Egyptian writing.[15]

One of the reasons Demotic was used by the Egyptians was because it was much quicker to write than Hieratic, and in turn the Hieratic was quicker than hieroglyphic picture writing. The same

---

15. The Rifaud Papyrus is an example of a largely undeciphered text. See *Bulletin de l'Institute Francais de'Archaeologie Orientale*, 50 (1952), pp. 107-117.

could be said for our system of writing. We can draw a picture of a horse, or print HORSE, or we can write *horse*. The latter, of course, is the fastest method and it is our present cursive style of writing. We also have shorthand, which is quicker still for those who are skilled in its use.

In an attempt to write the most they could in the least amount of space, reformed Egyptian was specifically chosen by the writers of the Book of Mormon. Mormon, the historian, wrote that he could have written more perfectly in the Hebrew but, because of a limited amount of space on the plates, he elected to use "reformed Egyptian."

Those who scoff at the idea of a "reformed Egyptian" script—written in the language of the Egyptians, yet after the learning of the Jews—would no doubt regard claims of an Aramaic text written in an Egyptian script in a similar light; yet such an item was found near Thebes. The papyrus was dated to the second century B.C. and scholars have determined that, although the text was written in the Egyptian Demotic script, the language itself was actually Aramaic.[16] (The text on this papyrus, by the way, gets its origin from the Hebrew Psalm 20.)

One more example of a language being written in another country's script is prevalent even today in the Coptic Church of Egypt and Ethiopia. They still preserve the native Egyptian language written in Greek letters.[17]

The characters on the metal plates of the Book of Mormon, referred to by Moroni as "reformed Egyptian," are now scientifically plausible, especially in light of the aforementioned verse stating that the composition of these characters incorporated a Hebrew influence along with the Egyptian. This group of Hebrews in America was acquainted with both of these languages before they left their homeland in Jerusalem, perhaps because of their occupations. LDS scholars have speculated that they were either merchants and/or metallurgists.

Conclusions

•Numerous writing styles have been found in ancient America. Some are related to Old World scripts.

---

16. Charles F. Nims and Richard C. Steiner, "A Paganized Version of Psalm 20:2-6 from the Aramaic Text in Demotic Script," *Journal of the American Oriental Society*, 103.1 (1983), pp. 261-274.
17. Cyrus H. Gordon, *Forgotten Scripts* (New York: Basic Books, Inc., 1982), p. 23.

•As was the practice of Book of Mormon writers, members of the priesthood in Mesoamerica were largely responsible for secret writing skills.

•There are six ways in which Egyptian and Mayan Hieroglyphs are related.

•A roller stamp from Tlatilco, Mexico, is similar in style to the transcript made from a plate of the Book of Mormon.

•Reformed Egyptian exists in several known styles and is not a singular oddity as anti-Mormon critics would have us believe.

Chapter 9

Wordprints, Chiasms, Hebraisms, and Codices

The authenticity of a written record can be determined, in part, by its literary forms. To substantiate the record in a scientific manner, it can be tested to determine the time period during which the record was used, approximately how many authors were involved in its writing, and with what culture were the writers most closely allied. On examination, the Book of Mormon's literary forms establish several facets of its authenticity.

Point

The Book of Mormon was written by prophets and historians of ancient America who had knowledge of both the Hebrew and Egyptian manner of writing, a manner which was modified and passed down to subsequent generations.

References: See for example: 1 Nephi 1:1, 2; Jacob 1:1; Enos 1:1; Jarom 1:1; 3 Nephi 1:2; Mormon 9:32-34.

Counterpoints

The Book of Mormon was highly original and imaginative fiction.[1]

Over 4000 changes had to be made in the Book of Mormon since it was first published in 1830.

What happens if questions are raised about the absurdities, grammatical errors, the contradictions, or the complete lack of archaeological evidence?[2]

Commentary

Many explanations for the authorship of the Book of Mormon have been offered by critics who do not accept the volume as inspired

---

1. Fawn Brodie, *No Man Knows My History*, 2d ed., New York (1971).
2. Ed Decker and Dave Hunt, *The God Makers*, Harvest House, Eugene, Oregon (1984), pp. 110, 114-115.

scripture written by prophets of God and other record keepers. If the record was written in the nineteenth century by one man—or several men—in collaboration, we should be able to determine this by examining the literary style of the work. If it was written by more than twenty authors (a claim made for the Book of Mormon) this also should become apparent in a careful study of the work. In other words, if it can be determined that there is multiple authorship, we will have a strong indication of the book's authentic ancient origin.

We also need to compare literary patterns in the Book of Mormon to ancient Hebraic prose. If the record on the metal plates is genuine, there will be strong similarities in the beginning of the account which will diminish as time progresses towards the end of the record. If we find this to be the case, we have additional evidence of the Book of Mormon's authenticity.

We also need to look for a geographical area in the Americas to coincide with the writing habits of Book of Mormon peoples. Which cultures were noted for keeping records—religious, historical, and genealogical? Which cultures kept books? If such an area can be found, we know we are right on target. In the nineteenth century, neither Joseph Smith nor his contemporaries were familiar with any of these methods of deduction.

Evidence

Corrections to the Book of Mormon

To date, over 3000 changes in later editions of the Book of Mormon have been made. The plates were orginally transcribed with very little punctuation and few paragraphs. There was almost no format: the text ran together so that it was almost impossible to reference particular sections or lines. Correct grammar was incorporated to clarify the book's meaning—not to change it.

All scriptures—whether the Old or New Testament, or the Book of Mormon—have undergone grammatical improvements in successive editions. The changes in the Book of Mormon, in particular, are conceptually insignificant. Hundreds of the changes made were merely to correct typesetting errors so that they would coincide with the original manuscript.[3]

---

3. See Paul R. Cheesman, *The Keystone to Mormonism: Little Known Truths About the Book of Mormon*, Deseret Book Company (1973), pp. 69-75; Stan Larson, "Changes in Early Texts of the Book of Mormon," *Ensign*, Sept. 1976, pp. 77-82.

A prime example of a justified change can be seen in a comparison of Helaman 3:23 between the 1830 and 1837 editions:

> . . . the secret combinations which Gadianton the *nobler* had established, in the more settled parts of the land. (1830 edition)

> . . . the secret combinations which Gadianton the *robber* had established, in the more settled parts of the land. (1837 edition)

Oliver Cowdery transcribed this section and the printer mistook Cowdery's "r" for an "n" and his "b" for an "l." The mistake was an innocent one but it needed to be set aright, as were similar mistakes made in many other verses.

It would have been inappropriate for spelling errors, made by writers who transcribed for Joseph Smith, to have remained. Many errors have been made by translators of the Bible, yet theologians continually make changes far more extensive than those made in the Book of Mormon. Thus, in some aspects, the present edition of the Book of Mormon may better reflect the intent of the original manuscript.

Wordprints

A variety of scientific tests have been done to prove the authenticity of the Book of Mormon. One of the most exciting of these tests done in our time is a result of the computer age: the wordprint.

The name "wordprint" has been coined by specialists in computer statistics to represent patterns of word usage which authors repeat in their writings—in other words, personal patterns of words.

An author's habits of style and literary form, for the most part, have only a slight variation over the years. A change in literary style is the exception—not the rule. Although some authors are not consistent in certain types of wordprints, this would not necessarily invalidate this concept. This is also typical of art. For example, Michelangelo was always Michelangelo, but Picasso changed his style periodically; yet an art historian would be able to tell you who did what, even if he never saw the work before, because of the regularity of expression.

What does this have to do with the Book of Mormon? If it could be determined that the Book of oMormon was written by a number of different authors, and that none of them used the style of nineteenth-century writers, then it could be said Joseph Smith did not write the book nor that the contents were a figment of his imagination.

Computer specialists Wayne Larsen, Alvin Rencher, and Tim Layton took upon themselves the massive task of assigning every word in the 1980 edition of the Book of Mormon to its speaker, or writer, as a preliminary step to the statistical technique they call "MANOVA (Multivariate Analysis of Variance). It is a complex computerized procedure used to compare Book of Mormon authors for statistical significance.

An oversimplified example is given by the team:

> Suppose we have three different passages from each of two authors. We find that they have used the word and with the following frequency:
>
>   Author A: .032 (32 times per thousand), .031, .032
>   Author B: .063, .065, .064
>
> We don't need any statistical training to understand that if the three selections from each author are typical, the authors are different in the frequency with which they use the word and.
>
> The MANOVA technique can examine any number of authors and any number of words. Based on the frequencies it analyzes, it evaluates the probability of different passages being the work of the same author.[4]

By comparing wordprints of different authors, these computer specialists determined several things: none of the selections resembled nineteenth-century writing styles, including that used by Joseph Smith; more than twenty individual writers were responsible for the compilation of books. They also determined that wordprints can be used to identify "a piece of writing as belonging to a particular author, just as a fingerprint or voiceprint can be traced to its originator."[5]

The amount of work done on this project (by these specialists) was certainly adequate to justify the results.

Other studies like this have been done to determine authorship of historical documents. Frederick Mosteller of Harvard University, and David L. Wallace of the University of Chicago, used computer analysis to determine the disputed authorship of "The Federalist Papers." By using wordprints, they were able to tell which papers were written by Alexander Hamilton and which were written by James Madison.[6] The method of computer analysis done by Mosteller and Wallace was primarily the same as that done by Larsen, Rencher, and Layton to determine Book of Mormon authorship.

---

4. Larsen, et al., "Multiple Authorship in the Book of Mormon," *New Era*, Vol. 9 (Nov. 1979), pp. 10, 11.

5. Wayne A. Larsen, Alvin C. Rencher, and Tim Layton, "Who Wrote the Book of Mormon? An Analysis of Wordprints," *BYU Studies 20* (Spring 1980), p. 243.

6. Frederick Mosteller and David L. Wallace, "Inference and Disputed Authorship: The Federalist," Reading, Mass.: Addison Wesley (1964).

Writing Styles

The differences in style between authors of ancient America and nineteenth-century men (Joseph Smith, Oliver Cowdery, and Sidney Rigdon, in particular), is considerable. Looking at the writings of some of the Book of Mormon historians, we can readily see a pointed difference in style between these men.

Dr. Robert Thomas has taken a close look at these variations.[7] For instance, he found that there is a marked difference in writing styles between the small books written by Enos, Jarom, and Omni.

Enos was impetuous—his sentences indistinct and fragmentary. "His words roll forth in an irresistible flood."[8] In Jarom, the next book in line, we see a drastic shift in style from that of Enos. Jarom is crisp, to the point, and yet there is a sereneness in his writing. He also takes the time to reflect on genealogies and Hebraic law. We see a literal, psychological contrast in the makeup of these two men.

Next is Omni. Again we find an author distinct and separate from both Jarom and Enos. Omni is a soldier: proud, dutiful, and perhaps a bit self-centered. In his first two verses he uses "I" seven times. His writings deal with war and peace, conquests and losses. He is not impulsive like Enos—he is not humble, yet forceful, as is Jarom.

If we must argue for the authenticity of the Book of Mormon, a personal study of the various writers of the Book of Mormon gives strong evidence of the book's individuality and, of course, its historic and authentic nature.

Chiasms

There are other types of criteria to show that the Book of Mormon is, indeed, a product of an ancient world. One analysis that can be made is a literary form called chiasmus which was prevalent in the writings of Hebrews as early as the eighth century B.C.

In simple terms, chiasmus is a poetic form or, in this case, scripture, wherein lines show an inverted relationship to other parallel lines. Some examples from the Bible would be:

---

7. Robert K. Thomas, "A Literary Critic Looks at the Book of Mormon," in *To the Glory of God*, Charles D. Tate and Truman G. Madsen, Deseret Book Company (1972), pp. 149-161.

8. *Ibid.*, p. 156.

Arise,
  shine;
    for thy light is come,
     and the glory of the Lord
      is risen upon thee.
       For, behold, the darkness shall cover the earth,
       and gross darkness the people:
      but the Lord shall arise upon thee,
     and his glory shall be seen upon thee.
    And the Gentiles shall come to thy light,
   and kings to thy brightness
  of thy rising. (Isaiah 60:1-3)

He that findeth his life shall lose it; and he that loseth his life for my sake shall find it. (Matthew 10:39)

Chiasms appear throughout the Book of Mormon, but they appear most frequently in the first half of the book; the years closest to the time this group departed from Jerusalem. A simple form of chiasms is the Book of Mormon would be:

That the Jews
  shall have the words
   of the Nephites,
   and the Nephites
  shall have the words
of the Jews. (2 Nephi 29:13)

It must be kept in mind that on the first page of the Book of Mormon the claim is made that the book was written "in the language of the Egyptians," but "according to the learning of the Jews." This would, of course, explain the use of chiasmus, a popular literary style of the Hebrews.

John Welch has thoroughly researched this particular aspect of the Book of Mormon.[9] He found the record full of chiasms ranging from simple phrases to very complex passages. With reference to the first work published on these parallelisms by John Forbes in 1854, Welch states: "No one in America, let alone in western New York, fully understood chiasmus in 1829. Joseph Smith had been dead ten full years before John Forbes's book was published in Scotland.[10]

---

9. See the following publications by John W. Welch: "Chiasmus in the Book of Mormon," *BYU Studies*, 10:1 (Aug. 1969), pp. 69-84; Masters Thesis, "A Study Relating Chiasmus in the *Book of Mormon* to Chiasmus in the *Old Testament*, Ugaritic Epics, Homer, and Selected Greek and Latin Authors" (May 1970); *Chiasmus in Antiquity*, John W. Welch, Editor, Hildesheim: Gerstenberg Verlag (1981).

10. Welch, "Chiasmus in the Book of Mormon," *ibid.*, p. 75

Of particular interest are the writings of Alma, a prolific writer, and a prophet in the Book of Mormon. The chapter of Alma 36 can be divided into three categories. In verses 1 through 5, Alma admonishes the people to obey the commandments and to trust in the God who delivered their ancestors from captivity in years past. Verses 6 through 24 tell of Alma's ordeal and the torment he experienced when he was a rebellious soul; then we read of the sharp contrast of the joy he found in accepting the Savior. Alma then begins to bring others to the church of God. In verses 26 through 30 we return to the first theme in an inverted literary parallel: trusting in God, receiving support and deliverance from God as in Egypt, keeping the commandments, and so on. The crux of this chapter is found at the center of the message in verse 17—revolving around Christ's atonement.

In our cited passages below, parallelisms can be found in the highlighted lines, comparing the first with the last and culminating at the center. As previously discussed, verse designations were not assigned at the time of the translation: in this study we must look at the literary chiastic construction of words and concepts.

Selected verses from Alma, Chapter 36:

1. *My son, give ear to my words;* for I swear unto you, that inasmuch as ye shall *keep the commandments of God ye shall prosper in the land.*

2. I would that ye should *do as I have done,* in remembering the *captivity of our fathers;* for *they were in bondage,* and none could deliver them except it was the God of Abraham, and the God of Isaac, and the God of Jacob; and *he surely did deliver them* in their afflictions.

3. And now, O my son Helaman, behold, thou art in thy youth, and therefore, I beseech of thee that thou wilt hear my words and learn of me; for I do know that whosoever shall put their *trust in God shall be supported in their trials, and their troubles, and their afflictions,* and shall be lifted up at the last day.

4. *And I would not that ye think that I know of myself*—not of the temporal but of the spiritual, not of the carnal mind *but of God.*

5. Now, behold, I say unto you, if I had not been *born of God* I should not have known these things; but God has, by the mouth of his holy angel, made these things known unto me, not of any worthiness of myself;

6. *For I went about* with the sons of Mosiah, *seeking to destroy the church of God;* but behold, God sent his holy angel to stop us by the way.

10. And it came to pass that *I fell to the earth;* and it was for the space of three days and three nights that *I could not open my mouth, neither had I the use of my limbs.*

14. Yea, and I had murdered many of his children, or rather led them away unto destruction; yea, and in fine so great had been my iniquities, that *the very thought of coming into the presence of my God did rack my soul with inexpressible horror.*

16. *And now, for three days and for three nights was I racked, even with the pains of a damned soul.*

17. AND IT CAME TO PASS THAT AS I WAS THUS RACKED WITH TORMENT, WHILE I WAS HARROWED UP BY THE MEMORY OF MY MANY SINS, BEHOLD, *I REMEMBERED ALSO TO HAVE HEARD MY FATHER PROPHESY UNTO THE PEOPLE CONCERNING THE COMING OF ONE JESUS CHRIST, A SON OF GOD, TO ATONE FOR THE SINS OF THE WORLD.*

18. Now, as my mind caught hold upon this thought, *I cried within my heart: O Jesus, thou Son of God,* have mercy on me, who am in the gall of bitterness, and am encircled about by the everlasting chains of death.

20. And oh, what joy, and what marvelous light I did behold; *yea, my soul was filled with joy as exceeding as was my pain!*

22. Yea, methought I saw, even as our father Lehi saw, *God sitting upon his throne, surrounded with numberless concourses of angels,* in the attitude of singing and praising their God; *yea, and my soul did long to be there.*

23. *But behold, my limbs did receive their strength again,* and I stood upon my feet, and did manifest unto the people that I had been born of God.

24. *Yea, and from that time even until now, I have labored* without ceasing, *that I might bring souls unto repentance;* that I might bring them to taste of the exceeding joy of which I did taste; *that they might also be born of God,* and be filled with the Holy Ghost.

26. For because of the word which he has imparted unto me, behold, *many have been born of God,* and have tasted as I have tasted, and have seen eye to eye as I have seen; therefore they do know of these things of which I have spoken, as I do know, *and the knowledge which I have is of God.*

27. *And I have been supported under trials and troubles of every kind,* yea, and in all manner of afflictions; yea, God has delivered me from prison, and from bonds, and from death; yea, and *I do put my trust in him,* and *he will still deliver me.*

28. And I know that he will raise me up at the last day, to dwell with him in glory; yea, and I will praise him forever, for *he has brought our fathers out of Egypt,* and he has swallowed up the Egyptians in the Red Sea; and he led them by his power into the promised land; yea, and *he has delivered them out of bondage and captivity* from time to time.

30. But behold, my son, this is not all; for *ye ought to know as I do know,* that *inasmuch as ye shall keep the commandments of God ye shall prosper in the land;* and ye ought to know also, that inasmuch as ye will not keep the commandments of God ye shall be cut off from his presence. Now *this is according to his word.*

The use of chiasmus was extremely popular in Hebraic literature, both oral and written. In fact, it was much easier to recite scripture and give oral presentations with the use of this form of rhetoric.
Alma was just one of the early American prophets who used this style,
and, it must be said, he used it extremely well.

Hebraisms

Another literary peculiarity that the Book of Mormon has in common with Old Testament writings are Hebraisms.[11] The frequent use
of the word "and," for example, is just one such Hebraism. The Hebrews
were particularly fond of starting a sentence with "and," as can be
seen in the opening chapters of the books of Ruth, Esther, Jonah,
Joshua, Judges, Ezekiel, and Exodus. We also find the early American Hebrews, who wrote the Book of Mormon, doing primarily the
same thing. The eleventh chapter of Alma has verses that begin with
"and" twenty out of twenty-three times.[12]

Examples from the Old Testament, Genesis 24:35, and the Book
of Mormon, Enos 1:21, are given below, respectively.

> *And* the Lord hath blessed my master greatly; *and* he is become great: *and*
> he hath given him flocks, *and* herds, *and* silver, *and* gold, *and* men servants,
> *and maidservants, and* camels, *and* asses.

> *And* it came to pass that the people of Nephi did till the land, *and* raise all
> manner of grain, *and* of fruit, *and* flocks of herds, *and* flocks of all manner
> of cattle of every kind, *and* goats, *and* wild goats, *and* also many horses.

Other Hebraisms used in the Book of Mormon, as well as in
Hebrew scriptures, would be the frequent use of words such as "his"
(his sons, his house, his cattle); "thy (thy children, thy flocks); "their"
(their inheritance, their goods), and so on. When it comes to a combination of the words "and it came to pass" the Book of Mormon reigns
supreme in the use of a Hebraic phrase. This phrase, in itself, is one
of the most conclusive proofs of Hebrew language structure found in
the Book of Mormon.

John Tvedtnes, a scholar of the Hebrew language, points out that
Book of Mormon expressions which are ungrammatical in English are,
in Hebrew, perfect grammar.[13] Some of these expressions that were

---

11. The literal translation into English of Hebrew words and parts of speech.

12. See "Hebraisms in the Book of Mormon," *The Zarahemla Record*, Issue Nos. 17 & 18, Summer & Fall (1982).

13. See "Hebraisms in the Book of Mormon: A Preliminary Survey," by John Tvedtnes, *BYU Studies* (1970) Vol. II, pp. 50-60.

present in the first edition of the book were subsequently changed to be more readable for an English-speaking audience. Nevertheless, the original does contain strong Hebraisms.

Tvedtnes gives us a prime example of how the original use of "that" and "which" were changed to the more comprehensive renderings of the pronoun "who" and "whom" in our current edition of the Book of Mormon. In Hebrew, the relative pronoun gives a literal translation from Hebrew to English for "that" and "which," as it was used for both humans and non-humans. These changes have caused Hebraisms to be lost, but there were times it was deemed necessary to make such changes to make passages more clear in the English language to which readers of the present are accustomed. This has also been done on numerous occasions in the Bible.

We are, once again, confronted with literary fingerprints from the Old World. It could be said that Joseph Smith was familiar enough with Hebraisms that he would use them, but even then, the perfection with which they appear in the Book of Mormon would be the result of an unlikely skill for a farmer to have, especially one with so little schooling. And there can be no question that complex literary concepts such as chiasmus would have been foreign to Joseph Smith in the nineteenth century frontier of western New York state. Indeed, there is only one explanation for the presence of these styles in the Book of Mormon: sound evidence that the Book of Mormon could not be a piece of fiction authored by Joseph Smith or any of his contemporaries. The ancient Israelite thread runs through this account with full force, only diminishing—in chiasmus in particular—towards the end of the account as would be expected after the authors of these accounts were so many years away from the land of their forefathers.

Codices

The Indians, as was evident in so many cultures of the Old World, were known for relating orally their genealogies, histories, and religious traditions. The Quiche Maya of the Guatemalan highlands also did this, as well as keeping records on bark that perished with time. After the Conquest, the Quiche Maya were urged to write these records in their language but using the European alphabet. The *Popol Vuh* was the result; it is deemed to have been derived from a native hieroglyphic manuscript already in their possession before the Conquest. As is stated in this sacred book of the Quiche Maya, "The original book, written long ago, existed, but its sight, hidden to the searcher and to the thinker."[14]

In the latest re-translation of the *Popol Vuh*, Munro S. Edmonson sees poetic parallel couplets used in the sacred texts of the Quiche.[15] This literary style is not far removed from the chiasms used among the Israelites of the Old World and as used in the Book of Mormon.

Of equal significance here is the content of the Mesoamerican storybooks (codices) and the Book of Mormon. According to the investigation made by Dr. John L. Sorenson, several similarities were found between these two types of ancient records.[16] For example, a relatively unknown priestly language was used in the codices. By the time of the Conquest, and probably for a considerable time before, only priests and some of the lords had knowledge of hieroglyphic writing. The same was true of Book of Mormon authors.

The subject matter of these accounts is also similar. Historical events evolving around a ruling lineage, and astrological systems affecting their lives, were the rule of thumb in these codices. The earlier Book of Mormon account is similar, but not as "pagan" in nature. For example, the Nephites record the history of their lineage (i.e., Jacob 1:2-3, 10-14), and the book is greatly concerned with prophecy, as revealed from the one God of all mankind. This is where there is a departure from similarity of the two records as the people fell away from their ancestors' beliefs, became polytheistic, and depended on astrological signs to predict their fate. Yet there is a pattern here, carried over from earlier times, adding still another evidence to support the authenticity of the Book of Mormon account.

Conclusions

•Grammatical changes in the Book of Mormon clarified the text— they did not change the meaning.

•The results of the MANOVA wordprint analysis indicate that the Book of Mormon was not a piece of fiction created by Joseph Smith.

•The wordprint testing was comprehensive enough to justify its conclusions.

14. *Popol Vuh*, Adrian Recinos (Normon: University of Oklahoma Press, 1975), pp. 79-80.

15. Munro S. Edmonson, "The Book of Counsel: The Popol Vuh of the Quiche Maya of Guatemala," *Tulane University, Middle American Research Institute Publication 35*, (New Orleans: MARI, 1971) xi-xiii.

16. See "The Book of Mormon as a Mesoamerican Codex," by John L. Sorenson, Newsletter and Proceedings, *Society for Early Historic Archaeology*, No. 139, December 1976.

•There are distinct variations in literary style between Book of Mormon authors.

•One literary style used by the ancient Hebrews was also used by early American prophets. This style is called Chiasmus.

•Hebraisms were used by Israelites in both the Old and New World.

•Ancient records of Mesoamerican peoples, called codices, have many similarities to the type of content covered in the Book of Mormon.

Chapter 10

The Ancient Ones

To the world at large, the sudden appearance of evidence of the first civilization in Mesoamerica remains a perplexing mystery. The identity and origin of these people are still unknown to most of the world, but the Book of Mormon clearly states who they were and where they came from. The Jaredite culture of the Book of Mormon and evidence found of the early Olmec peoples of Mesoamerica coincide extremely well.

Point

*A group of people, coined the Jaredites, left the Old World at the time of the Tower of Babel incident, coming to the Americas in eight seaworthy vessels. Their records were found by another group of Old World people and was eventually added to the record of the Nephites.

Reference: Book of Ether

Counterpoint

With reference to the Jaredites, Gordon Fraser states "a few contrary facts" which included:

No such civilization ever existed in America.[1]

Commentary

Ixtlilxochitl, a sixteenth-century historian, native of Mexico and of royal lineage, wrote that three groups of people came from across the ocean to populate Mesoamerica.[2] In his writings, the first group is referred to as the "Ancient Ones" and they are described as giants,

---

1. Gordon H. Fraser, *What Does the Book of Mormon Teach?* (Chicago: Moody Press, 1964), p. 90.

2. Ixtlilxochitl, Don Fernando de Alva, *Obras Historicas*, Alfredo Chavero, Editor, Editora Nacional, Mexico (1952).

or "men of large stature." The account of Ixtlilxochitl is important in light of what the Book of Ether states regarding the physique of these people. The brother of Jared, spiritual leader of these people, is referred to as "being a large and mighty man." This may not have been mentioned if he had not been exceptionally so.

Little is recorded in the Book of Mormon which is concerned with the history of the Jaredite people, but we do know that they eventually annihilated themselves as a nation through war, just as Ixtlilxochitl claimed was the fate of the "Ancient Ones" of the land.

Evidence

The Tower of Babel

Fray Diego Duran, a Dominican friar who lived thirty-two years among the Indians, kept fine records of legends, traditions, and histories of these people. He gathered his information from the wise and learned. He relates an interesting legend as told to him by an aged man from Cholula, Mexico.

According to tradition, the ancient men of the land were extremely large in size (this is in agreement with the account of Ixtlilxochitl). Desiring to reach the sun, they attempted to make passage to both the east and the west, but when they reached the sea they could go no further. As an alternative they "decided to build a tower so high that its summit would reach unto Heaven." The account continues true to Biblical form, asserting that "the giants, bewildered and filled with terror, fled in all directions."[3]

A Gnostic Hebrew sect, the Mandaeans, teach that at the time of the great wind, when the world was purged, the human race was splintered into many language groups. Their traditions speak of two men whose language was not changed: Ram and his brother Rud. These names are contractions—or shortened versions—of the original name. It would not be out of line to suggest that "Rud" may be our Jared. R. Eisler believes the name Rud means "wanderer," and Jared and his people were surely wanderers.[4]

---

3. Fray Diego Duran, *The Aztecs: The History of the Indies of New Spain*, translated with notes by Doris Heyden and Fernando Forcasitas, Orion Press, New York (1964), p. 5.

4. R. Eisler, *Iesous Basileus ou Baliseusas, Die Messianische Unabhaengigheitsewegung*, etc. Heidelberg (1930, II, n.l.).

Jaredite Ships

Those who are especially interested in marine navigation will find the construction of the eight Jaredite ships quite interesting. The book of Ether states that the ships were exceedingly tight "like unto a dish" (which we may assume is comparable to a covered bowl), and the ends thereof were peaked "and the length thereof was the length of a tree" (Ether 2:17). They were designed to have doors at both top and bottom which could be opened to obtain air (Ether 2:19). Were these and Noah's ark the first submarine-type vessels? Ether 6:7-8 states:

> And it came to pass that when they were buried in the deep there was no water that could hurt them, their vessels being tight like unto a dish, and also they were tight like unto the ark of Noah; therefore when they were encompassed about by many waters they did cry unto the Lord, and he did bring them forth again upon the top of the waters.

> And it came to pass that the wind did never cease to blow towards the promised land while they were upon the waters; and thus they were driven forth before the wind.

Now that we have access to translated Sumerian texts, we find a similar description of the Ark. It was called a "magur boat," written ideographically as *MA-TU*, which has a literal meaning of "a deluge boat." Like the Jaredite ships, it was specifically designed to be "driven by the wind." Seen from the side, it "resembled the crescent of the moon," an appearance which would coincide with the peaked ends of the Jaredite vessels. The Sumerian "magur" boats are further described by Hermann Hilprecht as follows:

> A solid lower part, strong enough to carry a heavy freight and to resist the force of the waves and the storm . . . the boat is called "a house" . . . which has a door to be shut during the storm flood . . . and at least one "air-hole" or "window."

> A "house-boat," expressed in the Hebrew story by an Egyptian loanword, "ark" originally meaning "box, chest, coffin," an essential part of which is its "cover" or "lid."[5]

Every aspect of the magur boat and the Jaredite vessels coincide, right down to the purpose of preserving those within even when the vessels were submerged.

---

5. H. V. Hilprecht, "The Earliest Version of the Babylonian Deluge Story," Vol. V Fasc. i of *Babylonian Expedition, University of Pennsylvania* (Philadelphia, 1910), pp. 51-55.

Luminous Stones

The ships of the Jaredites were described as tight "like unto a dish" with no source of light to illuminate the interior. To remedy this situation, the brother of Jared went to a mountain of great elevation and "did molten out of a rock sixteen small stones; and they were white and clear, even as transparent glass" (Ether 3:1). Because he had great faith, the brother of Jared turned to the Lord in fervent prayer. The account relates that the Lord granted his request by touching the stones and giving them luminosity. The brother of Jared then placed a stone at each end of both vessels: the stones gave off light sufficient for the passengers' needs.

We find a similar situation in the case of Noah; he, too, would have been in need of a source of light to illuminate the interior of the ark. *Tsohar* is the Hebrew word often used in the Old Testament when referring to light or windows.

> Many Jewish scholars of the traditional school identify *tsohar* as "a light which has its origins in a shining crystal." For centuries Hebrew tradition has described the *tsohar* as an enormous gem or pearl that Noah hung from the rafters of the ark, and which, by some power contained within itself, illuminated the entire vessel for the duration of the Flood voyage.[6]

Stones shining in the dark Jaredite vessels was not a novel idea invented by Joseph Smith. Accounts of similar illuminated stones can be found today in ancient records, but in the nineteenth century those records were not accessible to Joseph Smith or his contemporaries.

The above-reference *tsohar*, for example, comes to us from the Palestinian Talmud which, even in our time, is considered a rare and laborious book. The language of this particular Talmud is not English but the difficult West Aramaic dialect; only the most learned Rabbis ever read or cite it.[7]

The Olmec Civilization

In our search for archaeological evidence of the Jaredite nation, we must examine the early cultures of ancient America.[8] The Olmec civilization in Mexico would appear to be a good choice. Some of the oldest sculptures found in Mesoamerica belong to the Olmec people.

---

6. Rene Noorbergen, *Secrets of the Lost Races* (New York: Bobbs-Merrill Co., 1977), p. 46.

7. M. Mielziner, *Introduction to the Talmud* (1897), p. 62.

8. See *The Olmec World*, by Ignacio Bernal, University of California Press, for an excellent discussion of the Olmec culture.

Many have an affinity with those of ancient Mesopotamia, the homeland of the Jaredites. This would include sculptures relating to fertility where the lower half of the female figure is greatly exaggerated.

It is acknowledged that, in ancient times, some Asians used the Bering Strait land bridge as a passageway to the Americas. For many centuries, these people were known as food gatherers. We can, therefore, assume that the Mongolian strain was here before the races referred to in the Book of Mormon arrived. Yet something dramatic happened in the Americas with the advent of the "Ancient Ones," or the Olmec.

An unexplained aspect of Olmec society is the way it arrived on the scene in early times with an integrated culture. The "Ancient Ones" appear to have skipped the usual developmental stages between food-gathering and organized life and to have arrived out of nowhere in a state of full development.

The Book of Mormon gives us the explanation for this. The record informs us that the Jaredites came across the sea in eight seaworthy vessels containing all manner of seeds, birds, and animals. They also brought with them knowledge of the sciences as well as cultural developments of the Babylonians.[9] Thus we can say that, when the Jaredites arrived in ancient America, they arrived with a fully developed culture.

Linguistics

The study of linguistics is interesting. An especially interesting study is the comparison of Old World names and their symbolic meaning to similar names and symbols in the New World. We have already considered the name of Jared with its Old World counterpart. Several other Jaredite names are found in the Book of Mormon which appear to correspond with names of the Olmec period.

It has been suggested by Benjamin Urrutia, a graduate student in anthropology at the State University of New York, Albany, that two Jaredite names in particular, those of Shiblon and Coriantumr, have a bearing on Old World symbolism.

---

9. Maurice Chatelain, a NASA technician, suggests the basic calendar system of the Maya is similar to that of the Sumerians. Archaeologists have already established that the Maya received their calendrical system from the Olmec. In common with ancient Mesoamerican peoples, the Babylonians were the only ancient civilization that had a place value in their mathematics, the concept of zero. See *Nos Ancetres Venus du Cosmos*, by Maurice Chatelain, Paris: Robert Laffont (1975).

The element *shibl* means "lion cub" in Arabic. It thus parallels *corian*, an obvious cognate to Hebrew *gurion* "lion cub." Corianton should mean something like "the Lion Cub is Guardian."[10]

"Lion cub" would appear to be unusual for a man's name except among the Olmec: in their sculpture this animal reigned supreme. The lion is constantly encountered in the artistic works of the Olmec in the form of a jaguar—the nearest New World equivalent to the lion. The jaguar, as portrayed in figure 10.1 a and b, was held in high esteem by the Olmec. It was often portrayed as a human infant with jaguar-like features.

Fig. 10.1. (a) Stylized were-Jaguar celt, Olmec; (b) Typical were-baby jaguar, Olmec.

Both John A. Tvedtnes, a graduate student in Semitic linguistics and archaeology, and Robert F. Smith, a colleague of his, are of the opinion that proper names of the Jaredites, as recorded in the Book of Mormon, were drawn from the Akkadian and Sumerian languages, confirming the Mesopotamian origin of this early race in America. John Tvedtnes assures us:

10. Benjamin Urrutia, "Shiblon, Coriantumr, and the Jade Jaguars," *Newsletter and Proceedings of the S.E.H.A.*, No. 150, Aug. (1982), Provo, Utah.

The reader will notice that Joseph Smith, the professed discoverer and translator of the Nephite record in the 1820's, could not possibly have had knowledge
of those extinct Mesopotamian languages (they did not become known to
scholars until after the decipherment of the ancient cuneiform writing of
Mesopotamia in the mid-nineteenth century).[11]

Coriantumr

Coriantumr, last prophet of the Jaredite people, lived his remain-
ing days among another group, coined "Mulekites," who also came
from the Old World. Coriantumr related to them the story of doom
that befell his nation. It was through him that the record of his people, entitled the book of Ether, was passed on to the recorders of the
Book of Mormon.

It appears that the Olmec of Mesoamerica, and the Jaredites of
the Book of Mormon, are the "Ancient Ones" referred to by Ixtlilxochitl.
As far as can be determined according to the Book of Mormon, Jaredite history lasted approximately 1500 to 2000 years, ending around
500-300 B.C. This time period corresponds, with some flexibility, to
what archaeologists speculate was the length of time the Olmec culture thrived in Mesoamerica.

Conclusions

• The first grand culture of Mesoamerica, the "Ancient Ones," were
considered giants, or men of large stature. So were the Jaredites.

• These early Americans had knowledge of the Tower of Babel
incident.

• Some Jaredite names have their roots in Old World languages.

• The Jaredite vessels were similar in description to Sumerian boats.

• Luminous stones are referred to in the Palestinian Talmud as a
means to light Noah's ark.

• The Olmec culture seemed to arrive fully developed—out of
nowhere.

• The Olmec and Jaredite cultures fit historically into the same
time period.

11. John A. Tvedtnes, "A Phonemic Analysis of Nephite and Jaredite Proper Names," *Newsletter and Proceedings of the S.E.H.A.*, No. 141, Dec., 1977, BYU, Provo, Utah.

Chapter 11

Mulek and Company

If the Phoenicians reached the Americas in ancient times they may have brought with them Israelites from the Old World. One group reported in the Book of Mormon may have been involved in such a voyage.

Point

Shortly after the Lehi voyage to the "land of promise" (the American continent), another group from Jerusalem sailed to the same land, bringing with them a child named Mulek, son of the assassinated King Zedekiah. These people, referred to as the Mulekites, made contact with a Jaredite named Coriantumr.

References: 2 Kings 25:6.7; Helaman 6:10, 8:21; Mosiah 8; Mosiah 28:11.13; the book of Omni; Ether 15.

Counterpoint

It is one of the main contentions of Mormon theology that the American Indians are the descendants of the Lamanites and that they were of the Semitic race, in fact of Jewish origin.[1]

The Mulekite migration must have been attended by as many problems and hardships as the others, but no detail is given.[2]

Commentary

Although the Book of Mormon refers to several groups who migrated from the Old World, there is only one person in any of these groups who can clearly be identified as of Jewish origin—this is Mulek and, of course, any of his descendants. The Book of Mormon explains

---

1. Walter R. Martin, *The Maze of Mormonism* (Grand Rapids, Michigan: Zondervan Publishing House, 1962), p. 48.
2. Gordon H. Fraser, *What Does the Book of Mormon Teach?* (Chicago: Moody Press, 1964), p. 26.

who he was and gives some interesting highlights regarding his people's history.

Evidence

In about 200 B.C., a Nephite scouting party came across an unknown people in a land called Zarahemla. It was learned that these people arrived in the Americas shortly after Lehi's landing but in an area farther north.

This people told the history of their nation to the Nephites as best they could, for they kept no written records. Their history went back to a man called Mulek who was a son of King Zedekiah of Jerusalem. According to the Book of Mormon, at the time Zedekiah's family was assassinated (see 2 Kings 25:6-7), one son was rescued by a group concerned with his welfare. While Jerusalem was falling into the hands of her enemies, the rescuers of this young lad arranged for an escape to take him out of the city.

Hearing this account, the Nephites knew prophecy concerning Jerusalem had been fulfilled. It was for this very reason that Lehi took his family and left Jerusalem not too many years before the city's fall. Regarding this event, we read from the Book of Mormon, in Helaman 8:21, the following:

> And now will you dispute that Jerusalem was destroyed? Will ye say that the sons of Zedekiah were not slain, all except it were Mulek? Yea, and do ye not behold that the seed of Zedekiah are with us, and they were driven out of the land of Jerusalem?

The name "Mulek" is not mentioned directly in the Bible, but the late head of the Department of Archaeology at Tel Aviv University, Yohanan Aharoni, recently drew some interesting comparisons between the names Mulek and Malchiah regarding the name of Malchiah (Jeremiah 38:6). According to the King James translation of Jeremiah, Malchiah (in Hebrew—MalkiYahu, ben-hamMelek) was "the son of Hammelech." This clearly should have been translated "MalkiYahu, son of the King," since -melech in Hebrew means the same as melek, king. We now know that Malchiah was not just the son of an anonymous king but the son of Zedekiah.[3] In addition, it was a common practice during the sixth century B.C. to shorten names; i.e., the Old Testament name of Baruch, the prophet Jeremiah's scribe,

---

3. See *INSIGHTS: An Ancient Window*, Foundation for Ancient Research and Mormon Studies, Provo, Utah, June 1984, p. 1.

is a shortened version of his name *BerekYahu*.[4] It would not be out of line here to reduce Malchiah to something like "Mulek," as the son of Zedekiah is called in the Book of Mormon account.

Another point of interest lies in the Maya and Aztec calendar glyph, Muluc. In the world of the linguist, one would say "Muluc" has a close affinity to the word "Mulek." The calendrical day glyph, Muluc, corresponds to the Aztec symbol for water which may be significant since these people came across the waters to this new land in the Americas.

Of course the question arises, how did Mulek come to this land. The Phoenicians were of great service to the Hebrew nation in ancient times: they were the most skilled seafarers of their day. It has been suggested by some Book of Mormon scholars that Mulek came to the New World in a Phoenician ship. As a result of recent discoveries of stone inscribed with Phoenician characters (such as the aforementioned Paraiba inscription) we believe the Phoenicians reached the Americas. Whether or not they were hired to bring Mulek and his rescuers with them on one of their voyages is mere speculation but a very likely possibility.

In response to the lack of Mulekite history in the Book of Mormon, we need to look at two facts. First, the Mulekites admitted that they did not keep a written record of their history (Omni 17); what they knew was handed down orally from one generation to the next. If the Mulekites were, indeed, largely composed of Phoenicians, this would be even more understandable: the Phoenicians were noted for their lack of record keeping except for minimal amounts. Second, the Book of Mormon was written by the Nephites and was primarily concerned with Nephite genealogies and history. The story of the Mulekites continues in the Nephite record at the point when the two groups had their major first encounter.

It was during these first meetings that the people of Zarahemla (Mulek and friends' descendants) related to the Nephites what they knew of their history. Although the account is short, it is very significant. For example, according to the Book of Mormon, the Mulekites lived close to old Jaredite lands. Today several sculptures can be viewed in the areas of Mexico where the late Olmec culture once flourished.

---

4. Nahman Avigad of Hebrew University, Jerusalem, discovered the name BerekYahu (Baruch) on a seal-impression. See *Biblical Archaeologist*, 42:114-118.

The sculptures portray Semitic-type men with beards and aquiline noses.

The most important carving we have on this subject is the one so beautifully portrayed on Stela 3 at La Venta (figure 11.1). This monument has been designated the "Uncle Sam Stela" by the National Geographic Society. This fascinating story in stone depicts two races of people who appear to greet one another. Alexander von Wuthenau, an art historian, gives us his impression of this stela:

> The bold and energetic figure confronting us in such a realistic lively manner, radiating an almost cosmic intelligence, undoubtedly represents a prominent member of the Semitic group of people who once trod upon the ancient American stage.[5]

Tatiana Proskouriakoff, a staff member in archaeology at the Carnegie Institution, studied bas-reliefs in the area of La Venta and found "two racially distinct groups of people." She sees a "strong foreign component," especially among those groups that portray bearded strangers.[6]

Now if the Olmec are represented on the Uncle Sam Stela, both in the air in floating positions and on the left where we see one personage greeting another personage on the right, this may coincide with the story of the people of Zarahemla (Mulekites) greeting Coriantumr, one of the last survivors of the Jaredite people in that particular location (Omni 21).

It would also seem the implication here is that the Olmec (Jaredite) personages at the top represent a deceased race; one which has passed away: they are not earthbound. Yet one remains to greet a bearded foreigner, a man obviously from a Mediterranean race. This may yet prove to be one of the more significant stelae found to date to support a particular account in the Book of Mormon.

According to the Book of Mormon, the Mulekites had waned in their faith by the time they were found by the Nephites in approximately 200 B.C. Many of them adopted the theology of the Nephites, and the two cultures joined forces. In addition, a Nephite leader named "Mosiah" was proclaimed king of the united families of the Mulekites and Nephites.

5. Alexander von Wuthenau, *The Art of Terracotta Pottery in Pre-Columbian Central and South America* (New York: Crown Publishers, Inc., 1965), p. 131.

6. Tatiana Proskouriakoff, "Olmec and Maya Art: Problems of their Stylistic Relation," in E. P. Benson, Editor, *Dumbarton Oaks Conference on the Olmec*, Washington, D.C.: Dumbarton Oaks Research Library and Collection, Trustees for Harvard University (1968), pp. 121-123.

Fig. 11.1. "Uncle Sam" Stela 3, La Venta, Tabasco, Mexico. Reconstruction drawing, "Analysis of Two Low Relief Sculptures from La Venta," *Contributions of the University of California Archaeological Research Facility*, No. 3, pp. 25-55, Berkeley (1967). *Bottom left*, Close-up of Semitic dignitary enclosed in box. (Photo by Diane E. Wirth.)

Conclusions

•Of all the Book of Mormon cultures, only the Mulekites were of Jewish descent. The Phoenicians worked in close collaboration on several occasions with this tribe of Israel.

•The name Mulek means "the son of the king" which supports the premise that he is the son of King Zedekiah. Joseph Smith could not have known the interpretation of this word.

•The Mulekite history is not extensive in the Book of Mormon because they were not the record keepers of this book. Like the Phoenicians, the Mulekites did not keep a record of their history.

•Portraits of Semitic-type men have been located that may represent the Mulekite culture.

Chapter 12

Descendants of Joseph

Speculation about whether there were Israelites in pre-Columbian America was a popular subject during the nineteenth and early twentieth centuries. As a result of significant discoveries associated with Israelite traditions, many scholars now see the plausibility of these early theories.

Point

Lehi and his family claimed descent from Joseph of Egypt. It was Joseph's father, Jacob, who prophesied, in symbolic language, that Joseph's progeny would cross the waters to another land.

References: 2 Nephi 3:4, 5; Jacob 2:25; Alma 46:23; 3 Nephi 11:17.

Counterpoint

There is no evidence whatever of any migration from Israel to America, and likewise no evidence that pre-Columbian Indians had any knowledge of Christianity or the Bible.[1]

The Mormon apologists teach that the reference to "the fruitful bough by a well, whose branches run over the wall" refers to the incident of the family of Lehi crossing the ocean to America. . . . It would have been the method of the author, writing by the inspiration of the Spirit of God, to state that the progeny of Joseph would travel beyond the sea rather than to use the symbolism of a well or a wall to represent the idea of the ocean.[2]

Commentary

There is a great deal of evidence to support the theory of an Israelite (Old World) presence in ancient America.[3] In a general sense

---

1. Jerald and Sandra Tanner, *The Changing World of Mormonism* (Chicago: Moody Press, 1980), p. 145.
2. Gordon H. Fraser, *What Does the Book of Mormon Teach?* (Chicago: Moody Press, 1964), pp. 23, 24.
3. One of the best lists on the subject is published by the University of Texas Press, Austin (1971), in *Man Across the Sea*, edited by Carroll L. Riley, et al., in a chapter by Dr. John L. Sorenson entitled "The Ancient Near East and Mesoamerica."

we find, in the various writings of the Spanish fathers, the opinion that Indian rituals and customs were strikingly Hebraic and even Christian in derivation. Such traditions included stories resembling the Tower of Babel accounts in Hebrew lore and even an account of the exodus when the Israelites were supplied with manna from heaven.[4]

The blessing of Jacob to Joseph is of particular significance because it describes the future travels of a branch of Israel who would subsequently set foot on a land across the sea. Although this prophecy was given in symbolic language, this was the manner in which our Lord chooses to speak to his prophets throughout the ages. It was not out of line for a prophet to speak or write scripture in allegorical terms; in fact it was more in keeping with Hebrew tradition.

We will look at Joseph's blessing and the Israelite presence, both seen and unseen, in the Americas.

Evidence

Joseph's Blessing

Jacob's blessing to Joseph was short, clear, and precise (Genesis 49:22).

> Joseph is a fruitful bough, even a fruitful bough by a well; whose branches run over the wall:

Throughout the scriptures, branches often refer to individuals in a genealogical sense.[5] It is interesting to note that the people of pre-Columbian America also regarded the tree as an emblem of life and growth of a lineage or race. (See figure 12.1.)

When we examine Joseph's symbolic blessing as given above, the pieces fall together when we see the well as representing the ocean. The descendants of Joseph—the branches—would cross the waters and multiply their seed in a land on the other side of the sea.

As it is in many cases with duo-symbolism of words, "branches," in this case, may not only refer to members of a genealogical tree, but to a boat going over the wall of a well, or the sea. In the *Egyptian Book of What is in the Underworld*, the boat that travels in the waters of the underworld is called "Pa-khet" which, in English, translates as "branch."[6] The duo-symbolism in this prophecy may therefore refer

---

4. Lee Eldridge Huddleston, *Origins of the American Indians: European Concepts 1492-1729*, Austin, Texas (1967), pp. 38-39.

5. See for example Jeremiah 23:5, 33:15; Isaiah 11:1; Zechariah 3:8; and 2 Nephi 3:7.

6. E. A. W. Budge, *The Egyptian Heaven and Hell*, London (1906), Vol. I, pp. 47-48.

Fig. 12.1. Genealogical tree of the Xiu Family of Mani, the former ruling house of Uxmal. (Courtesy of Peabody Museum of Archaeology and Ethnology, Harvard University.)

not only to the seed of Joseph, in a genealogical sense, but to a boat which his seed would use to cross the waters.

To support this hypothesis, we look to Moses to further amplify this prophecy. Moses said to Joseph's seed that the land they were to inhabit would be "choice" and "bounteous." He further indicated that it would be in the "ancient mountains" and "lasting hills" (Deuteronomy 33:13-17). The land they would be led to would be a land of plenty and it would contain an extensive mountain range. This description aptly applies to the Americas. The western hemisphere is not only rich in food and minerals, but it does contain lasting hills, namely the Rocky Mountains which run through the western part of North, Middle, and South America.

In the Wilderness

The Book of Mormon deals primarily with the descendants of the tribe of Joseph through his son, Manasseh. According to their history this particular group of people began their journeys about 600 B.C. in the Near East. The records kept by their prophets in the Americas ceased to be written in approximately A.D. 421, when the account of their history ends—nearly 1000 years after these descendants of Joseph left Jerusalem for a promised land.

To corroborate the Book of Mormon in a physical sense, we must examine its history and look for corresponding similarities in both the Old and the New Worlds. One such account takes place early in the history of these people during their sojourn in the wilderness outside the boundaries of Jerusalem.

Lehi and his family were blessed with an unusual, divine gift. It was early in the morning when Lehi went to the door of his tent and found there an object of curious workmanship. The object, as described in 1 Nephi 16:10 and 26-30, was a ball encased in brass and having two spindles, or pointers, within it acting as directional devices or compasses. The Liahona, as they called it, was found to work only when it was used in their diligence and faith. This device guided them through the wilderness to a land they called Bountiful, near the seashore. Eventually the Liahona guided them across the ocean to the Americas.

The *Popol Vuh*, which contains a sacred history of the Quiche Maya of the Guatemalan highlands, and which was written from earlier sources shortly after the Spanish conquest, speaks of just such an object as the Liahona. In describing the migrations of their ancestors, the Maya claim that *Balam-Quitze* "left [them] the symbol of his being" and further instructed them that this object would be a source of power for their use. This symbol, or object, belonging to the ancestors of the Maya, was called the *Pizon-Gagal*.

Referring to the first people of the New World, H. H. Bancroft, a famous historian and recorder of Indian legends, wrote of a special object that was in the possession of their leader—an object that would appear to have produced the same results as the Liahona. Bancroft states:

It is not stated from whence they came, but merely that they came out of the regions where the sun rises. The supreme command was in the hand of the chieftain.

To his care was confided the holy envelope, which concealed the divinity from the human gaze, and he alone received from it the necessary instructions to guide his people's march.[7]

To understand the capabilities of this device we must look to another Maya manuscript, the *Title of the Lords of Totonicapan.* These Maya Cachiquel historians claim that Nacxit gave their progenitors, who came from the east, a unique gift called the *Giron-Gagal.* Like the Liahona, the *Giron-Gagal* was used as a directional device by their forefathers, and it was kept in what is referred to as a "sacred bundle." The record explains that, during their wanderings, they reported "we have not yet found the place in which we are going to settle," and that the Giron-Gagal was useful in aiding them to do so.

It is not implied here that the Liahona is the item referred to as the one that was kept in the sacred bundle. Still, it may have been an object that typified the characteristics of the Liahona. The capabilities of this object coincide well with the Book of Mormon account of the wandering of Lehi's family through the wilderness, under the direction of the Liahona, until they were led to the place they called "Bountiful." Both items appear to have had the function of a compass. Both were divine gifts from God.

According to Dr. Hugh Nibley, if we take syllable combinations and render Liahona as *le-yah-hon-na,* we come up with a literal translation from Egyptian to English:

"to God is our commanding," i.e., "God is our guide," since *hon, hwn,* is the common late Egyptian word for "lead, guide, take command."[8]

The Second Crossing

While they were in the beautiful land of Bountiful in the Near East, Nephi, the son of Lehi and favored of God, was instructed by

---

7. Hubert Howe Bancroft, *The Native Races,* Vol. III, (New York: D. Appleton & Co., 1875), p. 270.
8. Hugh Nibley, "The Liahona's Cousins," *Improvement Era* 64, (February 1961), p. 110.

the Lord to build a ship. Not unlike Noah, both the Jaredites and the people of Lehi were instructed to build seaworthy vessels of special design. (This is the second group of people recorded in the Book of Mormon to cross the sea to the Americas: the Jaredites were the first group.)

There are many curious legends concerning this particular group of people. John T. Short wrote of Clavigero's research of a branch of the Maya in Chiapas who spoke of a great man named "Votan." This leader's ancestors were involved in both the great flood and the disbursement at the time of the Tower of Babel. Dr. Short quotes from Clavigero:

> Votan came from the East, from Valum Chivin . . . from across the sea, by divine command to apportion the land of the new continent to seven families which he brought with him.[9]

As we will see in chapter 13, these seven families are of great significance to our story. Bancroft tells us about a culture-hero named "Votan" who came to America and apportioned the land among these seven tribes. Like Lehi, "he came by divine command . . . by sea from the east." He was responsible for building great cities; established ideas of religion and government; was a civilizer and law-giver; and, perhaps even more significant, he kept records wherein he wrote a "book in which was inscribed a complete record of all he had done."[10] Perhaps Votan is another name for Lehi or his son, Nephi, who were largely responsible for bringing these families to the New World.

Troublesome Brothers

The Book of Mormon frequently speaks of Nephi's troublesome brothers who often tried to abort the voyage and even harm their younger brother. However, they followed the counsel of their father, Lehi, and crossed the sea even though they were apprehensive about the trip.

The account written in the Book of Mormon regarding the early migrations of these people is unmistakenly reiterated in a Quiche Maya document entitled *Anales de los Xahil.* Before the natives arrived in this new land, they anxiously looked towards the sea and exclaimed:

> "It cannot be crossed. It has never been told that the sea has been crossed," said all the warriors of the seven tribes. "Who will tell us how we may cross the sea? Oh our younger brother, thou are our hope," they all exclaimed. . . .

9. John T. Short, *North Americans of Antiquity* (New York: Harper & Brothers, 1880), p. 204.
10. Bancroft, *ibid.*, Vol. V., p. 163-164.

"How shall we cross the sea, oh our younger brother?" they said. And we answered: "We shall cross in the ships. . . ." Then we entered the ships of the Ah Nonovalco; then we traveled eastward and arrived there.[11]

Bountiful = Tula

The capital city of the Nephite nation was "Bountiful," named after the fruitful land in the Near East from which their fathers came before sailing to the Americas. The Maya's *Popol Vuh* speaks of the time when their forefathers left a land named Tula in the Old World.

This we shall write now . . . the coming from the other side of the sea.

In Tulan power came instantly to them . . . They came, they pulled up stakes there and left the East. "This is not our home; let us go and see where we should settle," . . . And they wept in their chants because of their departure from Tulan. . . . The sign of the dawn they carried in their hearts when they came from the East and with the same hope they left there, from that great distance, according to what their songs now say.[12]

The Mexican word "Tula" (also Tulan or Tollan) has a similar if not identical meaning with that of "bountiful." According to the great historian, Sahagun, "Tulla" means "place of fertility and abundance."[13]

Even today there are ruins of a great city in Mexico called Tula, although this was not the original city of Bountiful. The ancient people of Mesoamerica are said to have built many Tulas, trying to recapture the glory that was once part of their ancient theocracy where the white and bearded god came to visit.[14] According to Aztec tradition, the city of Tenochtitlan (now Mexico City) was modeled after the lost capital of their original homeland in the New World. It is also said there were more than twenty cities in Mexico and Central America that bore the name of Tula. Whether they were successful or not we don't know, but we do know that they attempted many times over to duplicate the grandeur and spirit of this great city.

11. *Anales de los Xahil*, Traduccion y notes de George Raymond, Miguel Angel Asturias y J. M. Gonzales de Mendoza, National University, Mexico (1946).

12. *Popol Vuh, The Sacred Book of the Quiche Maya*, trans. Delia Goetz and Sylvanus Morley from Spanish translation by Adrian Recinos (Norman, Oklahoma: University of Oklahoma Press), 1950.

13. Fray Bernardino de Sahagun, *Historia General de los Cosas de Nueva Espana: Florentine Codex*, translated and edited by Charles E. Dibble and Arthur D. Anderson, Santa Fe: The School of American Research and the University of Utah (1950ff), in Prologue to Book VIII, II, p. 35.

14. See Chapter 14, "Jesus Christ in Ancient America."

The Narrative of Zosimus

Now that we have taken a look at some of the supportive evidence concerning the presence of Israelites in ancient America, including Book of Mormon peoples, we might relate some interesting material brought forth by John W. Welch in his article "A Book You Can Respect."[15]

While he was attending a graduate seminar at Duke University in North Carolina on the Pseudepigrapha, a body of ancient Jewish and Christian writings, Mr. Welch's professor presented an unusual and little-known text entitled "The Narrative of Zosimus."[16] Quoting from Welch's article in the *Ensign* regarding the contents of this narrative:

> It tells of a righteous family that God had led away from Jerusalem prior to its destruction by the Babylonians around 600 B.C. and how this group escaped to a land of blessedness where they kept records on metal plates soft enough that they could inscribe them with their fingernails. In the story, Zosimus was allowed to visit these people in vision. In order to get to their land, Zosimus had to journey through wildernesses, pass through impenetrable mists of darkness, cross the ocean, and come to a tree that bore pure fruit and gave forth water sweet as honey.

The similarity between the basic elements of the Zosimus manuscript and the account of Lehi and his family in the Book of Mormon is striking. The account of Zosimus's vision blends in well with this remnant of Israel in the Americas and suggests that early historians and theologians in the Old World were aware of such a migration from Israel.

Conclusions

•Joseph's blessing is perfectly logical in light of the fact that the prophets frequently spoke in allegorical language.

•Branches in ancient Israel were commonly known to represent genealogical lines. This symbolism was also popular in pre-Columbian America.

---

15. John W. Welch, "A Book You Can Respect," *Ensign*, Sept. 1977, Vol. 7, No. 9, pp. 44-48. See also John W. Welch, "The Narrative of Zosimus and the Book of Mormon," *BYU Studies*, Provo, Utah (1982).

16. "The Narrative of Zosimus" is published in English in Volume X of *The Ante-Nicene Fathers*, Allan Menzies, Editor, Wm. B. Eerdmans Publishing Company, Grand Rapids, Michigan. Two manuscripts of this account exist—one in Paris, the other in Oxford.

•It appears that knowledge of the Liahona was passed down to the descendants of the Lamanite and Nephite peoples since a similar device is referred to in Mayan histories.

•The ancient Maya knew their ancestors came from the east from a land whose name was comparable in meaning to Bountiful.

•*The Narrative of Zosimus* strengthens the validity of the Book of Mormon story since both the people and the plates were seen in a vision by a prophet of the Old World.

Chapter 13

The Seven Tribes

Who were the people who claimed ancestral ties to the ancient seven tribes of Mesoamerica? What was unique about their cultural background that enabled them to build civilizations in Mesoamerica that were superior, in many ways, to other pre-Columbian cultures in the Americas?

Point

Seven tribes, or lineages, are described in the Book of Mormon as having evolved from the families who came from Jerusalem to the New World.

References: Jacob 1:13 [circa 543 B.C.]; 4 Nephi 36-38 [circa A.D. 231]; and Mormon 1:8-9 [circa A.D. 323].

Counterpoints

Mormonism would gain a measure of respectability if only some credible evidence could be found to support at least one of Joseph Smith's claims.[1]

The bare facts of the matter are that nothing, absolutely nothing, has ever shown up in any New World excavation which would suggest to a dispassionate observer that the Book of Mormon, as claimed by Joseph Smith, is a historical document relating to the history of early migrants to our hemisphere.[2]

Commentary

Many theories have been proposed by LDS archaeologists and scholars to support statements made by Joseph Smith. The subject of the seven tribes in Mesoamerica has been of particular interest to this author and will be presented here as evidence to support the historical content of the Book of Mormon.

---

1. Ed Decker and Dave Hunt, *The God Makers* (Eugene, Oregon: Harvest House, 1984), pp. 86, 87.
2. Michael D. Coe, "Mormons and Archaeology: An Outside View," *Dialogue*, Vol. 8, No. 2 (Spring 1973), p. 46.

Not only were seven tribes of significant importance for hundreds of years among the Lamanite and Nephite nations, but a primary concern of Mesoamerican peoples was to trace their genealogies and prove their supremacy by declaring their descent from the lineage of the seven tribes.

Both the natives and early sixteenth-century Spaniards recorded histories of these people shortly after the Conquest: many of them state that the seven tribes came forth from seven caves. As will be seen, caves have a symbolic interpretation in Mesoamerican art and literature.

Evidence

Depending on their locale in Mesoamerica, different names for each of the original seven tribes are given in genealogical histories. These accounts are similar to those in the Book of Mormon in that their traditions not only refer to the seven tribes, but to the four that broke off from the original seven as well.

The seven lineages referred to in the ancient metal plates of the Book of Mormon split their allegiance. In general, the Nephites, Jacobites, Josephites and Zoramites[3] rallied under the name of the Nephites. The Lamanites took up the balance of the tribes; namely, the Lamanites, Lemuelites, and Ishmaelites.

There were times in their history when the seven tribes were united. During other periods, when wars were fought, the tribes became divided. An account written by the Cakchiquel Maya speaks of a time in their past when the tribes were united:

> Afterwards the seven tribes became fearful. . . . Did we not come with you to the east? Have we not come to seek our mountains and villages? . . . Thus spoke the seven tribes united in counsel.[4]

At other times the Cakchiquel Maya referred to just four tribes who were a split from the original seven.

> Thus, then, we were four families who arrived at Tulan, we the Cakchiquel people, oh, our sons! so they told us. . . . And these four branches which began were the tribes. . . . From the west we came to Tulan, from across the sea.[5]

---

3. The Zoramites fluctuated in their allegiance between the Nephites and Lamanites, but were originally allied with the Nephites and joined forces with them once again in later centuries.

4. *The Annals of the Cakchiquels*, translated from the Cakchiquel Maya by Adrian Recinos and Delia Goetz, University of Oklahoma, Norman (1974, 3rd printing), pp. 55, 56.

5. *Ibid.*, pp. 44, 45.

The Book of Mormon references given at the beginning of this chapter show the expanse of time in which the original seven tribes were remembered—actually, from the very beginning of their history to the end as recorded on the metal plates abridged by Mormon. Genealogy was extremely important to these Israelites as it was to pre-Columbian peoples. The Cakchiquels wrote, "And the glory of the birth of our early fathers was never extinguished."[6]

The *Popol Vuh*, the sacred and historical record of the Quiche Maya, speaks of their origins from the East. Their world was dark while they lived in seven caves but, during that time, they received guidance from the gods. They crossed the sea, using stepping stones (islands), and finally arrived in the new land.[7]

Coming forth from seven caves, boats, the underworld (womb of mother), etc., are all represented in myths of the "emergence," which legend is re-enacted even today among several Indian tribes. Let us examine the meaning of the seven caves in legend as well as in art.

Caves are of great significance in Mesoamerican symbology and must be understood in order to fully comprehend the tales told regarding the seven tribes. From the remotest antiquity in Mesoamerica, caves were closely associated with birth and creation. To a Mesoamerican's way of thinking, the darkness of a cave was comparable to the womb—the place of emergence. Many scholars feel the interior of a cave is symbolic of a ship's interior—the place from which the tribes emerged before setting foot on the western hemisphere.

This line of thinking is in accordance with what Bernardino de Sahagun had to say regarding this group of people.

> Concerning the origin of these peoples, the report the old men give is that they came by sea from the north, and true it is that they came in some wooden boats but it is not known how they were hewn, but it is conjectured by a report found among all these natives that they came from seven caves, and that these seven caves are the seven ships or galleys in which the first settlers of this land came, as gathered from likely conjectures.[8]

An ancient, detailed carving on a large boulder found near Santa Lucia Cotzumalhuapa, Guatemala, is an excellent portrayal of the seven tribes. (Figure 13.1.) The central figure of this illustrated story

---

6. *Ibid.*, p. 75.

7. *The Popol Vuh*, translated by Delia Goetz and Sylvanus G. Morely, University of Oklahoma Press, Norman (1950), Introduction pp. 63, 64, and *Popol Vuh*, third chapter.

8. Bernardino de Sahagun, *Historia General de las Cosas de Nueva Espana* (1946), Introduccion at Primer Libro.

Fig. 13.1. Artist's drawing, Monument 21, Bilbao, Santa Lucia Cotzumalhuapa, Guatemala. (Courtesy of Princeton University.)

in stone is, significantly, not of so-called Indian stock; his features are those of a Caucasian. Tied to his leg is an umbilical-type serpent rope which shows, in symbolic language, an ancestral tie—or bond—to the personage portrayed as a small head. This head, which is one of seven, is in a U-shaped enclosure that may represent a boat. In figure 13.2, water is seen spewing from a hole in the side of the vessel, almost certainly depicting the ancestral watery womb from whence these seven tribes emerged.

In Mesoamerica art, the U-shaped element is regarded as the symbol of the womb and, consequently, represents not only birth but the place of emergence, seen in figure 13.3. Donald Makenzie made the following observation.

Fig. 13.2. *Bottom right*, showing womb/boat element. Monument 21, Santa Lucia Cotzumalhuapa, Guatemala.

> The boat of the sun god is sometimes depicted as a U with a dot inside it. The mother goddess was the boat, and the boat was, apparently, her womb.[9]

Portrayed on this particular monument (figure 13.4)—the figure directly over our boat/womb symbol is none other than Ix Chel, the goddess of childbirth. Her sign of the twisted serpent atop her head easily identifies her as the mother goddess: she is often depicted, as she is shown in figure 13.5, throughout the land of the Maya. The U-shaped element below Ix Chel, containing the seven heads, has a spongy-looking texture composing the sides of this design and is representative of a mother's womb.

Four of the heads within the womb/boat enclosure are no doubt portrayed with symbols identifying their lineage. A flint knife and a bat are two examples. According to Zelia Nuttall, the flint knife,

---

9. Donald Alexander Makenzie, *Myths of Pre-Columbian America* (London: The Gresham Publishing Co., Ltd.), p. 201.

Tecpatl, was the symbol used to represent the supreme pontiff of one of the seven tribes.[10] The bat is also the emblem of one of the tribes. Ixtlilxochitl, a Chichimec king, claimed he was born in the Cave of the Bat.[11] The Cakchiquel Maya were also descended from the tribe of the bat; it was their tribal totem. This symbol is said to have been the tribal emblem in Chiapas from ages past.[12]

Fig. 13.3. Cave/womb design. After Codex Cuauhtlinchan.

Three of the heads within the enclosure of Monument 21 are known to be deified cocao pods: two of them have beards. (Cocao, valued as a means of currency, was highly regarded.) These three

Fig. 13.4. Mother goddess, Ix Chel. Monument 21, Santa Lucia Cotzumalhuapa.

10. See Zelia Nuttall, "The Fundamental Principles of Old and New World Civilizations: A Comparative Research Based on a Study of the Ancient Mexican Religious, Sociological and Calendrical Systems," *Archaeological and Ethnological Papers of the Peabody Museum*, Harvard University, (March 1901) Vol. II, p. 62.

11. See Charles C. Di Peso, *Casas Grandes a Fallen Trading Center of the Grand Chichimeca*, The Amerind Foundation, Inc., Dragoon Northland Press, Flagstaff (1974), Fig. 59-1.

12. *Annals of the Cakchiquels, op. cit.*, footnote 59, p. 59.

heads, or tribes, have no specific mark of identification. We suggest that this portion of the illustration refers to a division of the tribes: four representing the ancestors and relatives of the artist; the other three with their allegiance to the four severed.

Although Monument 21, at Santa Lucia Cotzumalhuapa, may prove to be a quite significant visual representation of the seven tribes, there are other representations of importance. Thomas S. Barthel suggests that a representation of the seven primordial earth-rulers is found on Stela 31, at Tikal in Guatemala.[13] An even clearer illustration of the seven tribes, labeled "Chicomoztoc," is found in the *Historia Tolteca-Chichimeca*. The English translation of Chicomoztoc is "the seven

Fig. 13.5. Ix Chel, wife of Itzamna and goddess of childbirth. Reproduced from *The Ancient Maya* by Sylvanus G. Morley, Stanford University Press (4th edition, 1983).

caves" and/or "the place of origin." Each petal of the flower-shaped design, seen in figure 13.6, represents a cave (womb), or tribe.

Analyzing the Chicomoztoc drawing, we note that two men at the lower right sport beards and wear priestly headdresses of quetzal feathers while the two men at the left, although beardless, are apparently associated with the symbol of the serpent. Quetzal feathers and the serpent are both known to be symbols of the white and bearded god of ancient America whose visit to the seven tribes is related in the Book of Mormon.

The *Book of Chilam Balam of Chumayel*, written by a Maya priest and copied from earlier codices and oral traditions, was originally in the language of *Zuyua*[14] considered to be the secret language of the priesthood. In chapter 8 it was noted that the Nephites used

13. See Thomas S. Barthel, "Die Stele 31 von Tikal," *Tribus*, Vol. 12 (1963), p. 209.
14. Ralph L. Roys, *The Book of Chilam Balam of Chumayel* (Norman, Oklahoma: University of Oklahoma Press (1973), pp. 88, 89.

Fig. 13.6. Chicomoztoc (seven caves), the place of emergence in ancient Mexican mythology. After illustration from *Historia Tolteca-Chichimeca*, Inah-Cisinah: Mexico (1976).

a unique language not known by other peoples of the land. It would, therefore, be of special significance if it can be proved that the language of the *Chilam Balam* had its roots in the seven tribes. Scholars confirm that the name *Zuyua* comes from the Nahuatl (Mexican heartland) and refers to the place of origin related to the "Seven Caves."[15] This is not to say that *Zuyua* was reformed Egyptian but that a secret language was a significant tradition held among descendants of the seven tribes.

One could say it is a coincidence that the seven tribes were mentioned in both the Book of Mormon and in native histories, but we must weigh the facts. Accounts by natives claim that their ancestors came from seven families from across the sea in a boat, or boats. They also believed in the white and bearded god whose name was never forgotten among their people.

Many of the races who claimed descent from these tribes have a high concentration of bearded figures in their work. Most of these nations were highly skilled and knowledgeable in the sciences as well as in writing skills and record keeping.

These are but a few of the similarities between the peoples who came from the seven tribes and the seven lineages referred to in the Book of Mormon account: too many similarities to be mere coincidence.

Conclusions

•The fact that many Mesoamerican tribes claim their descent from the seven tribes is just one more piece of evidence that adds to the lengthening list of correlations between Book of Mormon and pre-Columbian peoples.

•Genealogies were extremely important among both Old and New World cultures.

•Historical accounts relating the history of the Cakchiquel and Quiche Maya of Guatemala both refer to four tribes which were part of the original seven: so do the Nephites of the Book of Mormon.

•Several representations of the seven tribes have been found in both stonework and manuscript.

•The cave symbolized the tribal womb. It may also refer to a boat, or boats, in which the tribes came from the east across the sea.

---

15. *Ibid.*, Appendix E, p. 192.

Chapter 14

Jesus Christ in Ancient America

The legend of the white and bearded god who visited ancient America is retold, even today, by guides to thousands of tourists who travel through Mexico. The mystery of his identity is resolved in the Book of Mormon.

Point

After his resurrection, Jesus Christ came to the American continent to visit a remnant of Israel who left the Jerusalem area [circa 600 B.C.] for the "Land of Promise": the Americas.

Reference: 3 Nephi 15:21.

Counterpoints

In trying to find historical support for the Book-of-Mormon visit of Christ to America just after His resurrection, Mormons have grasped at the legends of Quetzalcoatl.[1]

The timing of the Quetzalcoatl legend is all wrong. The first mention of him in legend occurs about A.D. 1000. If he were indeed Christ, did all Indians just suppress the legend of the Messiah until then?[2]

Commentary

Many LDS writers have attempted to show a relationship between Quetzalcoatl, the white and bearded god of Mesoamerica, and Jesus Christ. As we shall see, there is a unique relation between this deity and our Savior.

This complex subject needs to be handled in a cautious manner. Our discussion will attempt to clarify confusion that has resulted in the past because the Quetzalcoatl tradition has been poorly understood.

---

1. Ed Decker and Dave Hunt, *The God Makers* (Eugene, Oregon: Harvest House, 1984), p. 196.
2. Latayne Colvett Scott, *The Mormon Mirage* (Grand Rapids, Michigan: Zondervan Publishing House, 2d printing, 1980), p. 79.

Evidence

Scholars agree that no other deity influenced the religious growth of the Aztec, Toltec, Itza, and Maya nations as much as did the white and bearded god who was known by various names in different locales according to their language.

Bancroft gives us a good understanding of what this deity meant to the natives of the land.

> And only Quetzalcoatl among all the gods was pre-eminently called Lord; in such sort, that when any one swore, saying, By Our Lord, he meant Quetzalcoatl and no other; though there were many other highly esteemed gods. For indeed the service of this god was gentle, neither did he demand hard things, but light; and he taught only virtue, abhorring all evil and hurt.[3]

Modern archaeological research, and the study of pre-Columbian books called "codices," open the door to help our understanding of the many puzzling traditions of the natives of Mesoamerica. We also rely on post-Conquest accounts written by Spanish chroniclers, but, since they often cause confusion, caution is suggested in the reading of these chronicles.

In the past, such confusion was the result of carelessly researched publications concerning Quetzalcoatl. Many investigators failed to make a distinction between the deity named Quetzalcoatl and later rulers who took upon themselves the name of their deity. More recently, several fine books have been published which unravel the Quetzalcoatl saga: they show clearly that there was, originally, the deity followed by many rulers who adopted his name.[4] These rulers took upon themselves the name of Quetzalcoatl as part of their own name much as the Moslems today take upon themselves the name of Mohammed.

Kukulcan is the Mayan name for Quetzalcoatl: both names are translated as "feathered-serpent." The tenth-century conqueror of Chichen Itza on the Yucatan Peninsula was named Kukulcan after the tradition of Romans, Egyptians, and other civilizations whose rulers, as has been stated, took upon themselves the name of deity. Consequently, this ruler's history is often confused with the deity Quetzalcoatl, whom he honored. Eduard Seler found an old description of Kukulcan which distinguishes him from the god he worshipped.

---

3. Hubert Howe Bancroft, *The Native Races of the Pacific States* (New York: D. Appleton & Co., 1875), Vol. III, p. 357.

4. For example, see *Quetzalcoatl and the Irony of Empire*, by David Carrasco, University of Chicago Press (1982).

Tozzer quotes from Seler's translation of an ancient manuscript of Motul: "Originally, a god had been worshipped here who was the creator of all things, and who had his dwelling in heaven, but that a great prince named Kukulcan with a multitude of people, had come from a foreign country, that he and his people were idolators, and from that time the inhabitants of this land also began to practice idolatry, to perform bloody sacrificial rites, to burn copal, and the like."[5]

Although Prince Kukulcan was known in his time as a governor, shrewd politician, and conqueror, he fell short of becoming like the kindly Quetzalcoatl of old. He was a very learned man in the science of astronomy and he had organized extensive trade in cotton and cocao. Today, at Chichen Itza, one can envisage the great empire Kukulcan helped to establish in the tenth century A.D.

Some authors assert that on the life of this particular dignitary the entire cycle of Quetzalcoatl legend was based. However, such a hypothesis is unwarranted. We now know there were earlier Quetzalcoatls (Kukulcans) who were more benign in disposition than was this Yucatanian conqueror.[6]

Ixtlilxochitl, the noted sixteenth century prince of Texcuco, had much to say regarding the virtues of one of the more kindly rulers who took the name of Quetzalcoatl:

And when they were in the height of their power, there arrived in this land a man whom they called Quetzalcoatl and others Huemac on account of his great virtues, considering him as just, saintly, and good; teaching them by deeds and words the path of virtue and forbidding them their vices and sins, giving laws and good doctrine.[7]

Getting back to the problem at hand: when we read the writings of the natives themselves, and those of the early Spanish historians, we find it difficult to reach the core of the Quetzalcoatl saga—it appears almost timeless. Even more difficult to sort out is a time period for the various Quetzalcoatls: the time when they lived. Does the historical source refer to a man who took upon himself this popular name, or does the record refer to the deity of Quetzalcoatl? We also have to account for mutations in the Quetzalcoatl tradition over the

---

5. Maud Worcester Makemson, a translation, *Book of Chilam Balam of Tizimin, The Book of the Jaguar Priest*, Henry Schuman, New York (1951), p. 117, cited in *Discoveries of the Truth*, by Diane E. Wirth (1978), p. 21.

6. See Carrasco, *op. cit.*

7. Don Fernando de Alva Ixtlilxochitl, *Obras Historicas*, Mexico (1891).

centuries as well as a possible "Christian gloss" added by over-zealous Catholic priests.[8]

It has even been suggested that some of the men who took upon themselves the name of Quetzalcoatl intentionally performed various acts in their lives according to the Quetzalcoatl tradition. By doing so, the impersonator became the image of the god, behaved like the god, and thus made history.[9]

The legends of Quetzalcoatl are so detailed that one is left with the impression that the legends were derived originally from the actions of a living person, rather than from legends given life through the imaginations of men. This is the picture that presents itself when we look at representations of the white and bearded god in Mesoamerican art, even prior to A.D. 350. For this reason, we must look back to the beginning of the Quetzalcoatl religion, even to the Book of Mormon, and then go forward to find remnants of that religion reflected in the religions we are more acquainted with because of their late date in Mesoamerican history.

When we turn to the archaeological record concerning the Quetzalcoatl tradition, the evidence is spectacular; representations of the feathered serpent are found throughout Mesoamerica. This symbol must, therefore, have been of great significance to these people. Let us try to understand why.

A literal translation of Quetzalcoatl is "feathered serpent," the name of the Aztec white and bearded god. The same is true of the Mayan name Kukulcan. This symbolic name is a beautiful combination of sky and earth: feathers represent a heavenly origin and the serpent an earthly one (figures 14.1 through 14.4). Because the serpent crawls on the earth, this deity was seen—in part—as a man of earthly origin; but, because feathers represent the air, Quetzalcoatl was also believed to be of heavenly origin. He was literally understood to be a man-god, as was Jesus Christ: son of an earthly mother and a heavenly father.

The ancient, universal concept of the serpent was largely one of divine wisdom; a symbol primarily used to represent the highest god in the heavens. The Greek *drakon*, "dragon," denotes the keen-eyed

---

8. An example of the human Quetzalcoatl would be legends referring to his drunkenness and/or conquests. Rites are usually associated with the deity rather than with one of his followers; and Spanish historians' allusions to the crucifixion of Quetzalcoatl on a cross would be considered a "Christian gloss."

9. Alfredo Lopez Austin, "Hombre Dios. Religion y politica en el mundo nahuatl," mimeographed thesis, UNAM, Mexico (1972), p. 103.

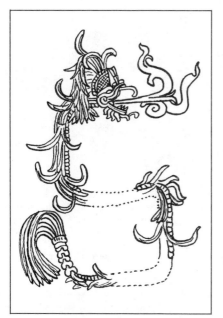

Fig. 14.1. The feathered serpent from Chichen Itza, Yucatan Peninsula.

Fig. 14.2. Quetzalcoatl, the feathered serpent. The priest within the mouth of the serpent shares the wisdom of this deity. (Housed at Museum of Anthropology in Mexico City.)

Fig. 14.3. The feathered serpent, Temple of Quetzalcoatl, Teotihuacan. (Photo by Diane E. Wirth.)

seer, as does the Sanskrit *Naga*, "serpent." According to the lxxxvii chapter of *The Book of the Dead*, the Egyptians believed "transformation into a serpent, implies wisdom and immortality and power of rebirth."[10] (See figure 14.5.)

Fig. 14.4. Feathered serpent frieze decorating the Temple of the Plumed Serpent at Xochicalco. (Note tail and head feathers and beard.)

A brass or bronze serpent on a pole was a representation of the hoped-for Messiah in ancient Palestine, and the serpent was kept on Solomon's temple until the temple was destroyed about 700 B.C. This parallel between Old and New World religious serpent-symbolism is striking and there is no doubt that the symbolism was maintained as a result of transoceanic voyages. The Book of Mormon relates that the Lamanite and Nephite people, whose history it records, were aware of the identification of the serpent with the Messiah (Helaman 8:13-15). This was evident to them through the writings they brought from the Old World: records of their ancestors written on brass plates.

The Book of Mormon tells us that Jesus Christ came to the Americas to visit a remnant of the house of Israel. At the close of the Book of Mormon period, about A.D. 385 (Mormon 6:22), the Nephites, who throughout their history were more highly devoted to the Lord's cause than any other group, fell into decadence. This, along with war, finally brought about the destruction of their nation.

What happened to the religion of Jesus Christ after the defeat of the Nephites? We know that not all the Nephites were killed; those who denied the Christ were spared by the Lamanites (Moroni 1:2). Did the religion die? Evidently not, because we find the symbol of the feathered serpent increasing in use right up to the time of the Conquest in A.D. 1519.

As time goes by, what we see in the history of these people is a gradual distortion of the gospel as it was known by them in earlier times. There was an increase in the number of gods, and the increase

---

10. See *The Secret of Ancient Egypt*, by Ernest G. Palmer (London: William Ridder & Son, 1924), p. 71.

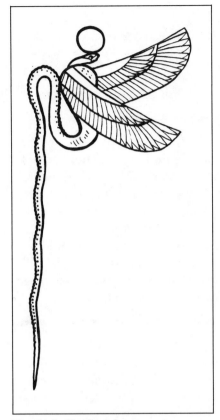

Fig. 14.5. Feathered serpent in a scene from the Egyptian *Book of the Dead.* (Reproduced after painting on papyrus, 21st dynasty.)

of human sacrifice had culminated in a great many deaths by the time the Spanish came. This certainly was not the church Christ established, so how do we know that the religion of Jesus Christ was remembered, even so remotely?

As time went on, Quetzalcoatl appeared in a new garb, wearing the guises of numerous deities whose various attributes were thought to reflect his personality. The similarities to the Christ-figure are so obvious that there simply can be no explanation other than that these later developments derived from the original, historical account of Christ in ancient America.

Let us look at these deities which were thought to incorporate the various aspects of the white and bearded god.

Ehecatl

Quetzalcoatl is closely associated with the elements of water and air. In his aspect as god of the air, Quetzalcoatl takes on the name of Ehecatl. Among the early natives, breath and air were considered one and the same. It was the lifegiving force itself that Ehecatl bestowed upon man.

Eduard Seler links Quetzalcoatl in his creator role with that of the wind god, stating that life is associated with the breath that emerges from the mouth, itself reminiscent of wind.[11] We are reminded here of the prophet Daniel's words, "and the God in whose hand thy breath is . . ." (Daniel 5:23).

---

11. Eduard Seler, *Gesammelte Abhandlungen zur Amerikanischen Sprach-und Altertumskunde,* 5 vols., Akademisch Druck Anstalt, Graz. (1960), Vol. IV, p. 142.

As Daniel Brinton so aptly puts it:

In the identity of wind with breath, of breath with life, of life with soul, of soul with God, lies the far deeper and far truer reason, for the prominence given to wind-gods in many mythologies.[12]

Lewis Spence speculates further with this interesting comparison:

It has been suggested that the Hebrew *Jahveh* (the archaic form of Jehovah) is connected with the Arabic *hawah*, to blow or breathe.[13]

Ehecatl is always depicted with a long, red-snouted mask which he used as a funnel to expel the wind or breath of life that Quetzalcoatl gave to man. Temples to this deity were unique in that they departed altogether from the pyramid-type characteristic to Mesoamerica. Round temples were erected in his honor, for as "The air goes all around the sky, thus the temple had to be round."[14]

Expanding on the concept of the god of the air being the god of creation, Laurette Sejourne, an archaeologist of great renown for her understanding of Mesoamerican religions, stated:

Moreover it is well known that the "maker of all creatures" was none other than Quetzalcoatl.[15]

The *Codex Borgia*, a pre-Columbian manuscript, gives a detailed and symbolic drawing (figure 14.6) of Quetzalcoatl in his role as the Wind God, Ehecatl, breathing life into a skeleton. In this image we see him in his creative function: the sign of life appears in the form of a heart emerging from the side of the skeleton. It is also here that we see this god in the role of one who, through resurrection, brings life to the dead.

The parallelism between Quetzalcoatl, in this aspect of the wind god, is so close to Christ's role as creator (Hebrews 1:2), and the one who is responsible for the resurrection of men (1 Corinthians 15:22), that we can only wonder at not only the similarity between the two, but at the plausibility that they are one and the same god.

---

12. Daniel G. Brinton, *Myths of the New World* (Philadelphia: David McKay, 1905), p. 69.

13. Lewis Spence, *The Gods of Mexico* (New York: Frederick A. Stokes Co., 1923), p. 115.

14. Bartolome de Las Cases, *Apologetica Historia de las Indias* (1875), chap. LI, p. 134.

15. Laurette Sejourne, *Burning Water: Thought and Religion in Ancient Mexico* (New York: The Vanguard Press), p. 40.

Fig. 14.6. Quetzalcoatl as the God of the air, Ehecatl, giving life to the dead. A living heart hangs from the rib cage of the skeleton. (After the Codex Borgia.)

Water Deities

On the Pyramid of Quetzalcoatl at Teotihuacan, Quetzalcoatl and Tlaloc appear side by side. They are companion gods and although both are sources of water, we find Tlaloc to be limited in his functions whereas Quetzalcoatl plays many other roles.

Both deities were associated with the symbol of the serpent. The snake with feathers, *quetzal-coatl*, moved not only in the waters of the earth but also moved in the waters of the heavens which are the clouds of rain. The root of the Mexican word Tlaloc, *Tlal*, is also the Semetic root for dew.[16] Jehovah of Israel, and Jesus Christ of the New Testament, were associated with life-giving waters and dew (Hosea 14:5; John 4:13-14).

---

16. John Phillip Cohane, *The Key*, Schocken Books (1976), p. 172.

Tlaloc often appears to wear goggles which, originally, were coiled snakes around his eyes. In his aspect of the rain god, Quetzalcoatl could become a tlaloc.[17] But Tlaloc was always Tlaloc and had no other function than those associated with rain and fertility, whereas Quetzalcoatl was strongly associated with baptism—an odd doctrine indeed, if we eliminate the concept of a Christian influence in Mesoamerica.[18]

Early Catholic missionaries, such as Bishops Landa and Sahagun, attested to the fact that baptism was a rite that existed long before the arrival of the Spanish. To quote Bancroft:

> It is related by all the old Spanish historians, that when the Spaniards first visited the kingdom of Yucatan they found there traces of baptismal rite; and, strangely enough, the name given to this rite in the language of the inhabitants, was *zihil*, signifying "to be born again." It was the duty of all to have their children baptized, for, by this ablution they believed that they received a purer nature, were protected against evil spirits and future misfortunes. . . . The rite was administered to children of both sexes at any time between the ages of three and twelve years.[19]

The design most closely associated with baptism was the shell which, by nature alone, represents water (figure 14.7). To the pre-Columbian aborigine, man emerging from a shell, portrayed in their drawings and sculpture as in figure 14.8, symbolized emergence from the womb to signify rebirth or baptism.[20] As illustrated in pre-Columbian codices, the importance of this symbol is strengthened by its frequent use on ornamental pendants worn by Quetzalcoatl.

Tlaloc never wore shell ornaments, and he participated strictly

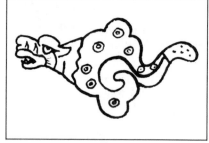

Fig. 14.7. Serpent shell motif from the Tonalamatl.

in rites that would promote rain. On the other hand, Quetzalcoatl's association with water appears to be of a spiritual nature.

17. Burr Cartwright Brundage, *The Phoenix of the Western World: Quetzalcoatl and the Sky Religion* (Norman, Oklahoma: University of Oklahoma, 1981), p. 155.

18. For a description of this baptismal rite, see Sejourne, *op. cit.*, p. 9-11. References to baptism in the Book of Mormon are extensive. Third Nephi 11:23-28, in particular, describes this ordinance and exactly how it is to be performed.

19. Bancroft, *op. cit.*, Vol. II., p. 682.

20. J. Eric S. Thompson, "Maya Hieroglyphic Writing," *Carnegie Institution of Washington*, Publication 589, Washington, D.C. (1950), p. 133.

Huitzilopochtli

Huitzilopochtli was one of the last deities to be created by Aztec priests. Even so, we see another dimension of Quetzalcoatl incorporated in this deity. Associated with the life-giving sun, often disguised as a hummingbird, he is a symbol of resurrection.[21] He is also associated with a ceremony which parallels the last supper, or passover, which Christ performed to symbolize his sacrifice.

Finding another Christian practice among these people causes Sejourne to comment:

> It is surprising to notice how, just as with baptism and the remission of sins, investigators have usually given only passing attention to the fact that the Mesoamerican [sic] peoples practiced the sacrament of communion.[22]

Fig. 14.8. Serpent god watches over man as he is reborn in the waters of baptism, Dresden Codex. (Bulletin 28, Bureau of American Ethnology, p. 428.)

A festival was held once a year among the Aztec wherein a statue of the god, Huitzilopochtli, was made of dough mixed with blood. The priests hurled a dart into the breast of the dough statue which fell when it received the stroke. After the dough was broken into pieces it was served to the male congregation.

We need only turn to 3 Nephi 18:1-9 to show the origin of the sacrament in the Americas. While Christ was on this continent, he demonstrated this principle to his disciples who, in turn, were commanded to give the same sacrament to the multitude.

Last generations of the Aztecs turned Huitzilopochtli into the patron deity of war. This is obviously a late development and a departure from earlier qualities assigned to this deity. Tradition even states that Huitzilopochtli was born of a virgin as was Quetzalcoatl and, of course, Jesus Christ.

---

21. The Aztecs believed that the hummingbird died during droughts and was resurrected at the beginning of the rainy season.

22. Sejourne, *op. cit.*, p. 61.

Sejourne confidently states her findings regarding the beginning of the Huitzilopochtli religion: "The roots of his symbolism must certainly have sprung from the very heart of Quetzalcoatl's doctrine."[23]

Xipe Totec

To associate Quetzalcoatl intimately with blood sacrifice who thus developed into a distinct deity took many centuries. Quetzalcoatl, in the guise of Xipe Totec, is typified as the sacrificial god. He it is whose skin is flayed in a sacrificial gesture for the sake of mankind.

Numerous scriptures in the Book of Mormon describe in great detail the meaning of the atonement.[24] The Book of Mormon was, of course, in very early times. Even though Xipe Totec evolved at a late date in pre-Columbian history, it does show that pre-Columbians had knowledge of the sacrifice of their god Quetzalcoatl. Describing this god, C. A. Burland states:

> It was thought that only through these sufferings were the gods induced to give mankind the blessing of the maize. He was thought of as a Lord of the Sunset, yet he always carried the staff through which he could see into the future. His was the function of sacrificing himself for the sake of the people and for the sake of all events in future time.[25]

There was a two-fold symbolism to the nature of Xipe Totec. Although his major function was to portray sacrifice, he was also considered the god of spring and resurrection. In this role he is associated with Quetzalcoatl.[26]

Spring is a time when new life bursts from the earth. In this light, Xipe Totec symbolized renewal of life as represented in the new skin under the torn flesh. When a priest who represented Xipe Totec wore the skin of a sacrificial victim, it was not meant to be a ritual of horror, but a symbol of rebirth and resurrection. (This interpretation of symbolism does not justify the actions of Mesoamerican natives, of course. It is merely used here to show that knowledge of a true principle once existed among these people—even though it was sadly distorted.)

---

23. Sejourne, *ibid.*, p. 157.

24. See in particular 2 Nephi 2:7, 20; 9:7, 26; and Mosiah 3:11.

25. C. A. Burland, *The Gods of Mexico*, Capricorn Books Ed. (1968), p. 137.

26. See Brundage, *op. cit.*, pp. 183, 184; and *The Toltecs*, by Nigel Davies, University of Oklahoma Press (1977), p. 61.

Xolotl

Xolotl is one of the most interesting, not to mention one of the more complex, of the Mesoamerican deities. This god was understood to be the larval form assumed by Quetzalcoatl while he was visiting the land of the dead. The functions of this god can readily be compared to Christ's visit to the deceased spirits in their prison, often referred to as the time when "he descended into hell" (1 Peter 3:18-20).

Sometimes Xolotl, figure 14.9, is depicted as a dog as in the *Codex Borgia*. His role is much like that of Pluto, the Greek "dog of Hades," and also like that of the dog-headed Egyptian god Anubis, who guided souls after their departure into the underworld. This would also be the same connotation we discussed earlier regarding figures of dogs on wheels that were buried with the dead.

This aspect of Quetzalcoatl was referred to as the twin brother of Quetzalcoatl. When he descended to the underworld to visit the dead, he offered a personal sacrifice by sprinkling their bones with this blood. When this was done, the skeletons of the dead were once more transformed into living men. This, of course, parallels with the atoning blood of Christ and the resurrection that is given to all men through his sacrifice.

Blood atonement in connection with the resurrection is not specifically referred to in the Book of Mormon, but there are several

Fig. 14.9. Xolotl, Quetzalcoatl in dog form, visiting dead of the underworld, after Codice Borgia.

scriptures which address the issue; i.e., man is delivered from spiritual and physical death as a result of Christ's preparing the way through his personal sacrifice (2 Nephi 9:11-13, 26).

Another aspect of this complex deity, Xolotl, was his heiroglyphic symbol of Venus. Legend tells us that after Xolotl journeyed to the underworld, he rose towards heaven in a resurrected state and became a god. As Quetzalcoatl and Xolotl are twins, or really two parts of one person, so was their symbol of Venus, the morning and the evening star.[27] That is, the planet Venus in the evening represented Xolotl on his way down to the underworld, while the morning star represented the resurrected Quetzalcoatl ascending to his throne on high. Tony Shearer, part Lakota Indian, writes of the evening star as follows:

> The Precious Morning Star, Sacred Twin, for he is also
> the Evening Star.
> He leads the Sun, at dawn, into the sky.
> And when the Great Sun has gone to sleep in the west,
> He, the Precious One, appears again as the Evening
> Star.
> Like the Moon, so Venus: a sign of rebirth, renewed
> life, return.
> Christ;
>   called himself the "Morming Star,"
> Quetzalcoatl;
>   was called the "Morning Star." . . .[28]

The true spirit of this deity could not be more beautifully expressed by one who understands the heart of the Indian and his beliefs, especially with regard to the symbol of Venus.

In the various aspects of Xolotl, there is yet another deity in the Mesoamerican pantheon of gods whose attributes are so Christ-like in their makeup that we cannot but pause to wonder at the many similarities.

The Christian Factor

The Aztec gods discussed in this chapter came from a long tradition of religious teachings of other cultures. The Aztec had no formal religion to speak of when they came to Tenochtitlan in Mexico. They were nomadic foreigners who, like the Phoenicians, adopted much of the religion and culture of tribes they conquered, even copying religious traditions from vacated areas. These doctrines included much of the Toltec and Mixtec traditions that lingered in both the Aztec's newly found lands and in neighboring areas. The ancient religion became so powerful among these newcomers to the land that it becomes obvious they knew in their very beings that the ancestors once living here were in possession of the truth. They wrote:

---

27. Brundage, *op. cit.*, p. 200.

28. Tony Shearer, *Beneath the Moon and Under the Sun* (New Mexico: Sun Publishing Company, 3d printing, 1981), p. 113.

> The plumes of the quetzal
>   the works of irridescent jade
>   all broken and gone
>   the memory of a beautiful world,
>   god-filled, truth-filled.[29]

Somehow, the religion of Jesus Christ, or Quetzalcoatl as he was known to these early Americans, was kept alive, perhaps by descendants of the Nephites and by others who adopted the faith. The purity of the gospel, however, was lost because of the corrupt manner in which these people chose to live. Yet we see so many Christian elements in their deities that we cannot ignore the plausibility factor of a true Christian influence in ancient times.

The gospel that was presented to them by Jesus Christ [circa A.D. 33] is preserved for us today in the Book of Mormon as recorded by early American prophets.

Conclusions

•Quetzalcoatl was a white and bearded personage/deity who came to the Americas in pre-Columbian times.

No other deity influenced the lives of the early Mexicans as much as did Quetzalcoatl.

•Quetzalcoatl was also a name adopted by men in an attempt to usurp his supremacy and thus gain the support of followers of this deity.

•The feathered serpent represented deity in both the Old and the New World.

Quetzalcoatl was emulated in and through numerous pre-Columbian deities.

•Like Jesus Christ, Quetzalcoatl is associated with creation, baptism, the sacrament of communion, sacrifice, descent into hell, and resurrection.

•The Book of Mormon gives us a comprehensive account of Christ's visit to these early American Israelites who were considered the sheep of his fold (John 10:16).

---

29. Victor W. Von Hagen, *The Ancient Sun Kingdoms of the Americas* (Cleveland, Ohio: World Publishing Co., 1961).

Index